بسم الله الرحمن الرحيم

آلْوَظِيْفَةُ الْكَرِيْمَةُ

A COLLECTION OF
PRAYERS & INVOCATIONS
(al-Wazīfat al-Karīmah)

BY SHAYKH AL-ISLĀM
IMĀM AHMAD RIDĀ KHĀN AL-QĀDIRĪ ﷺ

Collated, with invocations, by
SHAYKH MUSTAFĀ RIDĀ KHĀN ﷺ
&
SHAYKH IBRĀHĪM RIDĀ KHĀN ﷺ

Translated & Annotated by
Muhammad Kalīm al-Qādirī

MAKTAB-E-QADRIAH

Translation of *al-Wazīfat al-Karīmah* by Muhammad Kalīm al-Qādirī

Senior Arabic Editor: Abdul Aziz Suraqah
Manuscript Editor: Maryam Qadri

Published by:

Al-Mukhtār Books, US   &   Maktab-e-Qadriah, UK
PO Box 219 | Martinsville   29/30 Walnut St | Bolton
62442   BL1 8LN
info@almukhtarbooks.com   0044 1204 529740

Library of Congress Control Number: 2012904618
ISBN: 978-0-9831488-3-8

Cover Photo: A detail of the prayer niche in *Mezquita de Cordoba*, Spain. Copyright Adam Jones, Ph.D. Image sourced from flickr.com: http://www.flickr.com/photos/adam_jones/4616265678/

Please visit www.almukhtarbooks.com for more titles by and about the great Reviver of Islam, Imām Ahmad Ridā Khān al-Qādirī ﷺ.

Contents

Publisher's Notes

We have applied the following traditional honorifics using Arabic calligraphy and lettering:

ﷺ *sall-Allāhu 'alayhi wa sallam* (Allāh's blessings and greetings of peace be upon him) following the name of our Master, Prophet Muhammad ﷺ.

☀ *'alayhi as-salām* (peace be upon him) following the names of other Prophets ☀, Angels ☀, and Khidr ☀.

☀ *'alayhā as-salām* (peace be upon her) following the name of Maryam, Mother of Jesus ☀.

☀ *radīy-Allāhu 'anh/'anha* (may Allāh be pleased with him/her) following the name of a male or female Companion or Successor of the Prophet ﷺ, and the venerable scholar-saints of Islam [*al-Durr al-Mukhtār*, vol. 5/p. 480].

The Arabic text in *al-Wazīfat al-Karīmah* is accompanied by its English transliteration and translation so that non-Arabic speakers may recite the transliterated text, whilst meditating upon the meaning of each prayer. However,

vi

learning how to read the Arabic script and articulate the Qur'ān from a qualified teacher is not only advantageous in terms of becoming proficient in the correct recital of *al-Wazīfat*, but also a meritorious task in and of itself. We strongly encourage the reader to sit with those scholars following the well-trodden path [*maslak*] of Imām Ahmad Ridā Khān al-Qādirī ﷺ.

It has been our privilege to supplement the book with front and back matter that includes a Preface, Acknowledgements, an appendix on the *Dalā'il al-Khayrāt* entitled, "The Guidebook of Blessings," and a brief biography of the primary author, Shaykh al-Islām Imām Ahmad Ridā Khān ﷺ, and the authors of the additional invocations for success and salutations upon the Prophet ﷺ, namely, al-Muftī al-A'zam Shaykh Mustafā Ridā Khān ﷺ and al-Mufassir al-A'zam Shaykh Ibrāhīm Ridā Khān "Jīlānī Miyā" ﷺ. Commentary has also been provided to further elucidate certain points, and the chapters were rearranged in chronological order. Thus, the text begins upon waking and closes with "Salutations upon the Chosen One ﷺ."

Our hope is that the supplicant will read this book before sunrise, carry it with him throughout the day, and intone its eloquent litanies into the depths of the night.

Preface

It is said that Sultān Shihāb ad-Dīn Muhammad Ghorī (d. 602 AH/1206 CE) was so enamored by the wealth of India that he kept coming back to it despite seventeen unsuccessful attempts, until at last the great saint [*walī*], Khwāja Mu'īn ad-Dīn Chishtī ﷺ (d. 627/1230), gave him success. *Al-Wazīfat al-Karīmah* by Imām Ahmad Ridā Khān al-Qādirī ﷺ (d. 1340/1921) is no different. A seeker of knowledge, truth, and peace will not be able to resist its allure and keep coming back to it time and time again. In a similar vein, the blessings of A'lāhadrat[1] contained in this book will open for the wayfarer [*sālik*] untold spiritual wealth.

As is the wont of great saints [*awlīyā'*], they preach only what they practice and experience. There is no need,

---

[1] Imām Ahmad Ridā Khān ﷺ is referred to by many South Asian Muslims as A'lāhadrat (or, "The Great Presence"). He is a towering figure in the annals of religious renewal. According to historian Dr. Usha Sanyal in her biography on Imām Ahmad relations between center and periphery, Makkah the Ennobled and India, had been reversed during his second pilgrimage to the Haramayn in 1905, such was the stature of this remarkable scholar-saint. See Usha Sanyal, *Ahmad Riza Khan Barelwi: In the Path of the Prophet* (Oxford: Oneworld Publications, 2005), p. 73.

therefore, to argue the relevance of this book for it is based on the undisputed primary sources of the religion: the Holy Qur'ān and the confirmed Hadīth. *Al-Wazīfat al-Karīmah* is the Sunnah in practice. It is a practical guide for the believer [*mū'min*]. If the *sālik* sincerely applies its teachings he will traverse the stages of the path of wayfaring [*sulūk*] to Allāh Almighty by his spiritual state so that for him knowledge is experience.

O reader! The jewels contained within this book are precious beyond words and one cannot even hope to plumb their depths. It is my deep conviction that if you cleave to but one of these lost gems it will suffice you in this life and the next. May Allāh, the Exalted, grant us enabling success [*tawfīq*] to follow the guidance found within this publication and make it for us a means of salvation *on the day which will even turn the children hoary* (73:17),[2] āmīn.

Maryam Qadri
Al-Mukhtār Books
Rabī' al-Thānī 1433/March 2012

---

[2] *Hoary*: old and stale, white with age, covered with gray or white hairs.

The Translation & Acknowledgements

For the first time in more than a century, the Urdu masterpiece *al-Wazīfat al-Karīmah* (A Collection of Prayers & Invocations) by the Leader of the People of the Prophetic Way and the Majority of Scholars [*Ahl al-Sunnah wa al-Jamā'ah*], the Reviver [*mujaddid*] of the 14th Islamic century AH, the Lantern of Guidance, the Knower of Heavenly Realities, the Sea of Esoteric Secrets, A'lāhadrat Imām Ahmad Ridā Khān al-Qādirī ﷺ, is being brought forth into the English language.

I was first introduced to this book by my honorable father and teacher, Hadrat 'Allāma Muhammad Iqbal al-Qādirī al-Misbahī (may Allāh Most High preserve him) who knew it by heart. When the blessed month of Ramadān approached, he would walk from our house to the mosque reciting its invocations at the break of dawn. I would accompany him on these walks, and listen to him with rapt attention. Sometimes he would tell me the benefit of each *du'ā*. For instance, if one recites the final verses of Sūrah al-Hashr (59:21-24) then 70,000 angels supplicate for the reciter. According to a Hadīth narrated by Abū Hurayrah ﷺ, these *āyāt* also disclose "The Supreme Names of Allāh" [*Asmā Allāh al-'Izām*]. With such a powerful example, I was inspired to follow in my

x

father's footsteps by diving into this shoreless ocean with the intention of taking some of these beautiful pearls with me. Later, I was encouraged to translate this manual into English for the benefit of my English-speaking brethren here in the West.

While translating *al-Wazīfat al-Karīmah* I was mesmerized by some of the invocations collated by A'lāhadrat's beloved descendants, namely, al-Muftī al-A'zam Shaykh Mustafā Ridā Khān 🙏 (d. 1402/1981), and al-Mufassir al-A'zam Shaykh Ibrāhīm Ridā Khān "Jīlānī Miyā" 🙏 (d. 1385/1965), especially the latter's blessings and salutations [*salawāt*] upon the Beloved 🙏. Fearing these precious jewels might be lost I seized upon this golden opportunity and added them into this marvelous collection of litanies. The work of the former is found in the second to last chapter of this book, "Supplications for Success," whilst the statements of the latter comprise the final chapter, "Supplications upon the Chosen One 🙏."

I also felt a need to complete the provenance [*takhrīj*] of the Ahādīth cited for the prayers and invocations in *al-Wazīfat al-Karīmah*, thus—by the grace of Allāh Most High—the *takhrīj* for this work has been completed to the best of my ability. The reader will notice that I only give the primary references to each Hadīth in the "Translator's Introduction," but saved the detailed references for the book itself.

Many of the beautiful prayers and invocations have been transmitted from the noble Messenger himself 🙏, the early Muslims, the pious saints, and the august *Mashāyikh*. That is why *al-Wazīfat al-Karīmah* is like a necklace of gems.

If a Muslim strives to recite it like a rosary [*tasbīh*], then he will be able to invoke the All-Merciful One and earn His good pleasure. He will also experience firsthand the benefit of adhering to traditional formulae, as opposed to inventing one's own "sacred words." Hence, he will know directly that these supplications are particularly efficacious due to their connection with the chosen men of Allāh; these luminaries are linked to an authentic predecessor in an unbroken chain to the Leader of the first and the last ﷺ. Thus, it is an authoritative and authentic handbook.

Before concluding, it gives me great pleasure to thank my noble parents and teachers without whom this project would not have reached fruition. I also wish to thank the following individuals, who made this project a reality, our honorable friend and brother, Shaykh Abrar of Derby (UK), who helped in translating the formulae on sending blessings and salutations [*salawāt*] upon the beloved Prophet ﷺ, and especially to sister Maryam Qadri of al-Mukhtār Books (US) who copyedited the manuscript, added useful comments, and gave beneficial feedback. The latter, together with her husband (Ghulam Dastagir), also designed the front and back cover and spent tireless effort typesetting the book to produce this masterpiece as it appears before you.

May Allāh the Exalted reward each and every one of them in both worlds and grant them all a prosperous life full of happiness and joy, āmīn. May the Lord of Truth accept this humble effort from us and preserve it as a treasure [*dhākhira*] on *the day when neither wealth nor sons shall profit, except for him who comes to Allāh with a pure heart* (26:88-89).

May the Sublime Lord shower countless blessings and salutations upon the Master of the Messengers, the Best of Creation, the Chosen One, our liege-lord Muhammad, and upon his noble Family and illustrious Companions, and those who follow them righteously, āmīn.

Muhammad Kalīm al-Qādirī
Maktab-e-Qadriah
Bolton, UK
Rabī' al-Awwal 1433/February 2012

A COLLECTION OF
PRAYERS & INVOCATIONS
(al-Wazīfat al-Karīmah)

Translator's Introduction

By Muhammad Kalīm al-Qādirī

بسم الله الرحمن الرحيم

الحمد لله رب العالمين والصلاة والسلام على سيد الانبياء والمرسلين و
على آله و صحبه اجمعين

In the Name of Allāh,
the Most Gracious, the Most Merciful

All praise belongs to Allāh alone, the Lord of the worlds.
Peace and blessings be upon the Master of the Prophets
and Messengers, and upon his Family and Companions.

This small but very significant book is a collection of
selected supplications [du'ās] from the Qur'ān and the
Hadīth compiled by A'lāhadrat Imām Ahmad Ridā Khān
al-Qādirī ﷺ. The author did not wish to burden his readers
with references. Thus, he wrote a popular work that
would be handy to every Muslim from the local butcher to
the Chief Judge [Qādī al-Qudāt]. Being an erudite scholar
and an adept spiritual physician, he wrote the perfect
prescription for today's spiritual aliments that will ensure
the removal of cares, Insha'Allāh. His eldest son, Hujjat al-

1

Islām Shaykh Hāmid Ridā Khān al-Qādirī ❀, collated what had already been compiled, and gave it a fitting name, *al-Wazīfat al-Karīmah*. He then published it for the benefit of the *Ahl al-Sunnah* brethren.

It seems as though A'lāhadrat Imām Ahmad Ridā Khān al-Qādirī ❀ intended to adorn this book with additional supplications and litanies [*awrād*], but his appointed time had come on Friday, the 25th of Safar, 1340 AH (October 28, 1921). In consequence, the project was left incomplete until the author's beloved son, Shaykh Hāmid Ridā ❀, uncovered it among his father's personal effects. Realizing he had unearthed a precious gem, he immediately put the finishing touches on his father's parting gift. The purpose of this collection of supplications [*du'ās*] is to keep reciting it as a litany [*wird*]; but to derive maximum spiritual benefit from the *awrād* the reader must strive to memorize it. His tongue should be moist with it and his heart enlivened by its constant reverberation.

Even a cursory glance at this concise book of supplications [*du'ās*] reveals that A'lāhadrat Imām Ahmad Ridā Khān al-Qādirī ❀ had carefully selected the most effective *du'ās* for diurnal activities, with special emphasis given to the day and night. This was done for the purpose of extending daily benefit to the entire Community [*ummah*]. He also included brief notes on the benefit of each supplication to facilitate the reader in the acquisition of knowledge. However, it has come to our attention that some readers require a more detailed commentary, and would like to see full references for each supplication cited. Thus, a humble effort has been made to fulfill their request to the best of our ability by adding commentary with additional footnotes for further elaboration, as and when necessary. Readers are encouraged, of course, to forgive any oversights on our part and bring these to our attention.

ALL HIS NAMES ARE BEAUTIFUL (17:110)

A litany (*wazīfah* in Urdu and *wird* in Arabic) is the name given to those authentic formulae used for the remembrance of Allāh Most Pure [*adhkār*], while supplications [*du'ās*] are special supererogatory prayers offered by an individual on a daily basis. Shaykh Abu'l Mahasin Muhammad ibn Khalīl Qāwuqjī ﷺ in his commentary[3] on a famous litany by Shaykh Muhyi'd-Dīn ibn 'Arabī ﷺ eloquently said:

والورد يطلق على معان بطريق الاشتراك إطلاقا أصليا أو مجازيا
على أن أصله النوبة فى ورود الماء سمى ما يجعله المرء على
نفسه من قراءة أو صلاة أو غير ذلك وردا تشبيها بذلك و يقال له
حزب أى طائفة من الأذكار أو جند كما فى قوله أولائك حزب
الشيطان أى: جنده و نصيب لان قارئه جعله حظه أو اخذ نصيبه، و
سلاح كأن من قرأه جعله سلاحا يدافع به

"*Wird* is an Arabic word that has multiple meanings, because it is spelled or pronounced in the same way as one or more other words, either in its original sense or metaphorically. In its original

---

[3] See *at-Tawr al-Aghla fi Sharh ad-Dawr al-A'lā li-Sayyidī Muhyi'd-Dīn ibn 'Arabī*, p. 5.

3

sense it means 'taking turns in arrival at a watering
hole,' whilst its metaphorical meaning is fixing a
time (and place) for reading a portion of the Holy
Qur'ān or performing one's daily devotions. This is
also called *wird*, because of its similarity to the
original meaning, which refers to a daily repetitious
action. It is also referred to as a group [*hizb*] as in 'a
group of litanies,' or an army [*jund*]. This [word]
has been mentioned in the Qur'ānic verse: *They are
from Shaytān's army [jund]*. It also means 'a weapon'
[*silah*], since it will become a weapon for the one
engrossed in the remembrance of Allāh so that he
might defend himself [spiritually from the
onslaught of evil]."

Whenever and wherever one makes mention of his
Sustainer and remembers Him and engages in His
remembrance [*dhikr*], he will attain reward and his *du'ās*
and prayers will be answered. Religious authorities have
given a great deal of importance and extolled the
excellence of authentic forms of invocation [*adhkār*]. They
have also praised those supererogatory invocations that a
person carries out on a regular basis, regardless of the
quantity, for our Prophet ﷺ has said:

احب الاعمال الى الله ادومها و ان قل

"The most beloved of all actions in the sight of
Allāh are those that are carried out consistently,
even if little in amount." (Related by al-Bukhārī,

Muslim, and al-Khatīb at-Tabrīzī ﷺ in his *Mishkāt al-Masābīh*.)

Furthermore, Allāh Most High states:

فَٱذْكُرُونِىٓ أَذْكُرْكُمْ وَٱشْكُرُواْ لِى وَلَا تَكْفُرُونِ ۝

"Then remember Me; I will remember you. Be grateful to Me, and reject not faith." (2:152)

This means that Allāh the Exalted has completed His favor upon us by sending to us His noble and beloved Messenger ﷺ and through him, teaching us the Book and Wisdom [i.e., the Holy Qur'ān and Ahādīth]. Hence, we must be grateful to Him for these miraculous blessings and everlasting bounties, and remember His rights over us, and refrain from being ungrateful.

The benefit that we receive from this is that Allāh Most High remembers us in front of His elite servants and remembers us in the loftiest of gatherings. What greater honor can there be for an inferior bondsman than to be remembered by his Master, his Creator, his Cherisher? Indeed, those who are remembered by Allāh Most High are blessed with eternal bliss, felicity, and protection from all physical and spiritual calamities in this life and the next.

CATEGORIES OF DIVINE REMEMBRANCE

There are three categories of divine remembrance [dhikr]:

1. *Dhikr bil-Lisān* is verbal remembrance with the tongue. This means to glorify Allāh, extol Him, and praise Him audibly. Sermons [khutbahs], repentance [tawbah] and seeking forgiveness [istighfār] are also included in this category of remembrance.
2. *Dhikr bil-Janān* is remembrance of the heart. This means to contemplate and ponder upon the countless blessings of Allāh Most High, to consider the manifest signs within His creation which signify His Majesty, Sublimity, and Oneness. A scholar of sacred knowledge [mujtahid], who practices *ijtihād* or qualified legal reasoning, also falls under this category of *dhikr*.
3. *Dhikr bil-Jawārih* is physical remembrance and obedience through the limbs. A prime example is to perform the Pilgrimage [Hajj] to the ennobled city of Makkah.

Ritual prayer [salāh] is the most comprehensive form of *dhikr*, because it includes all of the aforementioned types of remembrance. For instance, glorifying Allāh Most High [tasbīh], magnifying His greatness by saying: "Allāhu Akbar (Allāh is the Greatest)" [takbīr], praise [thanā], and the recitation of the Holy Qur'ān [qirā'at]. These are integral acts in *salāh* and an excellent form of verbal remembrance [*Dhikr bil-Lisān*]. Whilst being in a state of absolute neediness before the Master of the Realm [*Mālik al-Mulk*] and sincerely turning to Him with gratitude and humility is remembrance of the heart [*Dhikr bil-Janān*]. Simultaneously, one engages in remembrance of the limbs [*Dhikr bil-Jawārih*] through adopting the various postures of the prayer such as standing [*qiyām*], bowing [*rukū'*], and prostration [*sujūd*]. 'Abdullāh ibn 'Abbās ❀ gave the following interpretation to the aforementioned verse (2:152), "Allāh the Exalted says, 'Remember Me' through obedience; and 'I shall remember you' through assistance."

It has been narrated in a Hadīth that Allāh Most High states:

إِذَا ذَكَرَنِي عَبْدِي خَالِيًا ذَكَرْتُهُ خَالِيًا، وَإِذَا ذَكَرَنِي فِي مَلَإٍ ذَكَرْتُهُ
فِي مَلَإٍ خَيْرٍ مِنَ الْمَلَإ الَّذِي ذَكَرَنِي فِيهِ

"If My servant makes mention of Me to himself, then I make mention of him to Myself, and if he remembers Me in a gathering, then I shall make mention of him in a gathering superior to his." (Related by at-Tabarānī ❀ in his *al-Mu'jam al-Kabīr* and al-Bazzār in his *Musnad*.)

In the same way 'Abdullāh ibn 'Abbās ❀ related that the Messenger of Allāh ❀ said:

قَالَ رَسُولُ اللهِ صَلَّى اللهُ عَلَيْهِ وَسَلَّمَ : " يَقُولُ اللهُ تَعَالَى : يَابْنَ
آدَمَ إِنْ ذَكَرْتَنِي فِي نَفْسِكَ ذَكَرْتُكَ فِي نَفْسِي ، وَإِنْ ذَكَرْتَنِي فِي مَلَإٍ
ذَكَرْتُكَ فِي مَلَإٍ أَفْضَلَ مِنْهُمْ وَأَكْرَمَ

7

"Allāh Most Exalted states, 'O son of Adam! If you remember Me secretly, I remember you in-kind. And if you remember Me in an assembly, then I make mention of you in an assembly loftier and more virtuous than yours.'" (Related by at-Tabarānī in *al-Mu'jam al-Kabīr* and Diyā al-Maqdisī in his *al-Ahādīth al-Mukhtārah*.)

The excellence of performing *dhikr* has been mentioned in numerous verses of the Holy Qur'ān and narrated time after time in the Ahādīth. All types of *dhikr* whether by the tongue, by the limbs, or even silently [*khafī*] are virtuous in the sight of Allāh, the Exalted.[4]

Allāh Most High mentions the excellence of performing *dhikr* in abundance. Yet we neglect His remembrance in this modern day and age. In fact, those who engross themselves in an abundance of *dhikr* are made targets of derisive laughter. Contemporary Muslims tend to look down upon sincere seekers for not being worldly. It is disheartening to see Muslims shy away from remembering their Lord in abundance, because this is a one of a kind gift that necessitates Divine succor and felicity in this life and the next. Allāh Most High states:

---

[4] Imām 'Abd al-Wahhāb al-Sha'rānī has dedicated a separate chapter on continuously remembering Allāh audibly [*jahr*] and in secret [*khafī*] so that one reaches a state of always being in the presence of the Almighty (*Lawāqih al-Anwār al-Qudsiyyah fī Bayān al-'Uhud al-Muhammadiyyah*, pp. 203-208.)

لَّقَدْ كَانَ لَكُمْ فِى رَسُولِ ٱللَّهِ أُسْوَةٌ حَسَنَةٌ لِّمَن كَانَ يَرْجُواْ ٱللَّهَ وَٱلْيَوْمَ

ٱلْأَخِرَ وَذَكَرَ ٱللَّهَ كَثِيرًا ۝

*"You have indeed in the Messenger of Allāh a beautiful
example (of conduct) for anyone whose hope is in Allāh and
the Last Day, and who engages much in the praise of Allāh."*
(33:21)

This verse informs us that Allāh Most High has made
His noble Messenger ﷺ an ideal role model for us.
However, only those who affirm their belief in Allāh, the
Last Day, and praise Him abundantly will follow the
Sunnah of our Master Muhammad ﷺ successfully. With
abundant *dhikr*, a man molds his heart by softening it. He
remembers the day of accounting, and becomes hopeful of
Allāh's Mercy, thus it becomes easier for him to follow in
the footsteps of the noble Messenger ﷺ. Indeed, this is but
one of the great benefits that a Muslim shall reap from
excessive *dhikr*. Our pious forebears held gatherings of
dhikr for this reason, and many fortunate people still do to
this day.

Allāh Most High reiterates the importance of *dhikr* to
Prophet Zakariyyā ﷺ with the words:

قَالَ رَبِّ ٱجْعَل لِّى ءَايَةً قَالَ ءَايَتُكَ أَلَّا تُكَلِّمَ ٱلنَّاسَ ثَلَثَةَ أَيَّامٍ إِلَّا

رَمْزًا ۗ وَٱذْكُر رَّبَّكَ كَثِيرًا وَسَبِّحْ بِٱلْعَشِىِّ وَٱلْإِبْكَرِ ۝

9

"... then celebrate the praises of thy Lord again and again, and glorify Him in the evening and in the morning." (3:41)

We are to remember Him frequently by performing His *dhikr* in the morning and evening. In the same way, Allāh Most High said to our noble Prophet ﷺ:

$$وَٱذۡكُرِ ٱسۡمَ رَبِّكَ وَتَبَتَّلۡ إِلَيۡهِ تَبۡتِيلًا ۝$$

"But keep in remembrance the Name of thy Lord and devote thyself to Him whole-heartedly." (73:8)

We are to remember Him alone and engage ourselves whole-heartedly in His remembrance. Or it means that whenever we remember Him, do so with full concentration and with complete devotion and utmost humility whilst having severed all ties with this world. To have one-pointed attention on Allāh alone is a great right that we must strive to fulfill when we perform *dhikr*.

DHIKR IN DIRE SITUATIONS

The importance of *dhikr* can also be understood by the fact that even in dire situations where one is overcome with fear he is commanded to remember Allāh. For example, Imām al-Husayn ﷺ, the martyr of Karbalā, lost his life while performing the ritual prayer in the midst of battle. His throat was parched, his family and children were mercilessly slaughtered, and yet he engaged in the highest of all forms of *dhikr* forfeiting his own life and preferring the remembrance of the Allāh, the Exalted, and the life to come. The Holy Qur'ān states:

$$يَـٰٓأَيُّهَا ٱلَّذِينَ ءَامَنُوٓا۟ إِذَا لَقِيتُمْ فِئَةً فَٱثْبُتُوا۟ وَٱذْكُرُوا۟ ٱللَّهَ كَثِيرًا$$

$$لَّعَلَّكُمْ تُفْلِحُونَ ۝$$

"O ye who believe! When ye meet a force, be firm, and call Allāh in remembrance much (and often); that ye may prosper." (8:45)

When confronted by a force, Allāh Most High has commanded us to be firm, and make His *dhikr* in abundance as He alone is the All-Powerful. If one neglects this vital duty and merely relies on the apparent means, then he is bound to falter before his enemy, and he will not remain steadfast in battle. One of the greatest factors that contribute to our weakened state is that we have completely relied upon this material world and forsaken the real source of our strength. Cars, businesses, property, wealth etc. preoccupy our thoughts. We have become incredibly heedless of the One, Who has no partner, Who is the Sustainer of the heavens and the earth. The real origin of a believer's power and his strength is his reliance upon Allāh as it is only His remembrance that revitalizes the withered heart of a believer and it is through His remembrance that an anxious heart finds peace. Only *dhikr* can bring solace to a broken heart and mend a troubled world. Allāh Most High states:

11

ٱلَّذِينَ ءَامَنُواْ وَتَطْمَئِنُّ قُلُوبُهُم بِذِكْرِ ٱللَّهِ ۗ أَلَا بِذِكْرِ ٱللَّهِ تَطْمَئِنُّ ٱلْقُلُوبُ

۞

*"Those who believe, and whose hearts find satisfaction in the
remembrance of Allāh: verily in the remembrance of Allāh do
hearts find rest." (13:28)*

It is inevitable that hearts waver and are overcome
with fear and apprehension in the midst of conflict. But at
such times only the *dhikr* of Allāh can fill our hearts with
peace, tranquility, courage, and self-assurance. Muslims
must habituate themselves to *dhikr*. We must be in the
constant habit of praying, reciting the Holy Qur'ān, and
reading litanies. Otherwise, when confronted with
misfortune, hardship or injustice, we will forget our Lord,
turn on our heels, and behave badly much to our chagrin.
We must fight against our lower self [*nafs*] in the midst of
the day to day grind by remembering Him as much as
possible.

Contemporary Muslims are desperately seeking peace.
We are trying to buy happiness and time. Yet we end up
increasing our stress and anxiety, whilst hurrying to be
late to prayers, bed, school, and work. We are living in a
hurried world. What the Prophet ﷺ mentioned fourteen
hundred years ago is happening today: "Truly among the
Signs of the Last Days are that time will contract,
knowledge will decrease, shortages and miserliness will
become prevalent, afflictions will appear, and there will be

much *harj*. The people asked, 'O Messenger of Allāh, what is *harj*?' He said, 'Killing, killing!'"[5]

Time *will* contract; in the past a journey to Makkah the Ennobled took several months, and there was a distinct possibility of a loved one dying along the way. But today, a Muslim can make that same trip in less than twenty-four hours with little to no hardship involved. Our great-grandparents rode in bullock carts or horse draw carriages to reach a neighboring locality, yet many of us commute to work often traveling to entirely different cities in an hour or less. Materialism expects us to earn more and do more with very little time, and we naturally feel a tremendous amount of pressure to perform and succeed. We forget about why we're here, what we're living for, and ultimately how to worship our Lord in a truly meaningful way. We try to "pursue happiness," when in fact it is a state of mind. It is a condition of the soul, not a commodity that we can buy and sell.

Although this might sound like a tall claim in the face of life's realities, it is a time tested fact, which the noble Prophets and scholar-saints of our grand tradition have proven through their own spiritual states: The secret to felicity, patience, truthfulness, contentment, good moral character, absolute trust in Allāh Almighty and success in this life and the next rests in His remembrance. Other methodologies available on the consumer market are merely gimmicks. These quick "fixes" take the traveler

---

[5] Shaykh Muhammad Hisham Kabbani, *The Approach of Armageddon? An Islamic Perspective* (Washington: Islamic Supreme Council of America, 2003), p. 107.

nowhere and enable our spiritual malaise to fester and grow. It is for this reason that we are constantly reminded by our Merciful Lord to make mention of Him, to remember Him, to engross ourselves in an abundance of *dhikr* in every state, in every field, in every step of our lives.

فَإِذَا قَضَيْتُمُ ٱلصَّلَوٰةَ فَٱذْكُرُواْ ٱللَّهَ قِيَـٰمًا وَقُعُودًا وَعَلَىٰ جُنُوبِكُمْ فَإِذَا ٱطْمَأْنَنتُمْ فَأَقِيمُواْ ٱلصَّلَوٰةَ ۚ إِنَّ ٱلصَّلَوٰةَ كَانَتْ عَلَى ٱلْمُؤْمِنِينَ كِتَـٰبًا مَّوْقُوتًا ۝

"When ye pass (the congregational) prayers, celebrate Allāh's praises, standing, sitting, or lying down on your sides; but when ye are free from danger, set up regular prayers: for such prayers are enjoined on believers at stated times." (4:103)

Even after having performed the ritual prayer [*salāh*], which is the highest form of *dhikr* one should not be heedless of his Lord. Thus, the command is given that even after completing the obligatory ritual prayer [*salāh*] a Muslim must continue to perform *dhikr* in all states and conditions such as standing, sitting, or lying on his side. When we fail to do this Shaytān disquiets us through his whispering, until at last we are overcome by negative emotions that readily hurl us into a condition of sin. Most, if not all, of our social and spiritual ills are due to a lack of *dhikr*.

14

'Abdullāh ibn 'Abbās ﷺ said, "Allāh Almighty has set a limit for each obligation save His *dhikr*; there is no limit to it. That is why we have been commanded to perform *dhikr* whilst 'standing, sitting, or lying on our sides,' during the night and in the day, whether on land or at sea, at home or abroad, in sickness and in health, in public [gatherings] or in private."[6]

Performing the litany [*wird*] of the testimony of faith, "There is no god, but God (*lā ilāha illa'llāh*)" after each ritual prayer [*salāh*] is deduced and established from the aforementioned Qur'ānic verses and Ahādīth. Moreover, the testimony of faith [*kalimah*] has been decreed, "The most virtuous form of remembrance [*afdal ad-dhikr*]" by the Prophet ﷺ himself,[7] which is why the *Mashāyikh* recite it as part of their daily routine and keep it as their constant *wird*. As well as the testimony of faith [*kalimah*], words of glorification [*tasbīh*], magnification [*taqdīs*] and exaltation [*takbīr*] are all included in *dhikr*. The Glorious Qur'ān says:

$$\text{قُلِ ٱدْعُوا۟ ٱللَّهَ أَوِ ٱدْعُوا۟ ٱلرَّحْمَٰنَ ۖ أَيًّا مَّا تَدْعُوا۟ فَلَهُ ٱلْأَسْمَآءُ ٱلْحُسْنَىٰ}$$

$$\text{وَلَا تَجْهَرْ بِصَلَاتِكَ وَلَا تُخَافِتْ بِهَا وَٱبْتَغِ بَيْنَ ذَٰلِكَ سَبِيلًا}$$

"Say: 'Call upon Allāh, or call upon Rahmān: by whatever Name ye call upon Him, (it is well): for to Him belong the most beautiful Names. Neither speak thy prayer aloud, nor

---

[6] See *Khazā'in al-'Irfān* by Shaykh Na'īm ad-Dīn al-Murādabādī.
[7] Narrated by at-Tirmidhī and Ibn Mājah.

speak it in a low tone, but seek a middle course between.'"
(17:110)

This verse clearly stipulates that whatever name we call upon in *dhikr* is in accordance with the Holy Qur'ān and Sunnah. By the same token Sūrah al-Ahzāb also reiterates the importance of *dhikr* and stresses upon the amount that should be performed:

يَـٰٓأَيُّهَا ٱلَّذِينَ ءَامَنُوا۟ ٱذْكُرُوا۟ ٱللَّهَ ذِكْرًا كَثِيرًا ۝ وَسَبِّحُوهُ بُكْرَةً وَأَصِيلًا

۝

"O ye who believe! Celebrate the praises of Allāh, and do this often. And glorify Him morning and evening." (33:41-42)

This verse not only stresses the importance of *dhikr*, but also mentions that we should be glorifying Allāh during the morning and evening [e.g., by saying: "Glory to God" (*Subhān Allāh*)"]. First, we are given a general command to "do this often" and then Allāh the Exalted specifically reminds us to glorify Him "morning and evening," which may indicate that we should constantly perform *dhikr*, or perhaps it means specifically at those times, as the angels who record our deeds change shifts in the morning and evening, so they will take this *dhikr* (or the lack thereof) to the court of Allāh Most High.

16

ADDITIONAL BENEFITS OF DHIKR

Another great benefit of performing *dhikr* is that it softens
and transforms the heart; hence, a believer's heart will
become concerned with the hereafter and gradually sever
its ties and attachments to this mundane world. Whereas,
a hypocrite [*munāfiq*] feels agitated at the mention of *dhikr*
and flees from it, or he recites beautifully but its taste is
bitter. Unveiling this truth, Allāh Almighty states:

إِنَّمَا ٱلْمُؤْمِنُونَ ٱلَّذِينَ إِذَا ذُكِرَ ٱللَّهُ وَجِلَتْ قُلُوبُهُمْ وَإِذَا تُلِيَتْ عَلَيْهِمْ

ءَايَٰتُهُۥ زَادَتْهُمْ إِيمَٰنًا وَعَلَىٰ رَبِّهِمْ يَتَوَكَّلُونَ ۞

*"For believers are those who, when Allāh is mentioned, feel a
tremor in their hearts, and when they hear His Signs
rehearsed, find their faith strengthened, and put (all) their
trust in their Lord." (8:2)*

And again in Sūrah al-Hajj the Almighty commands us
to give glad-tidings to the humble. He describes them as
those whose hearts tremble in fear when His Name is
mentioned.

وَلِكُلِّ أُمَّةٍ جَعَلْنَا مَنسَكًا لِّيَذْكُرُوا۟ ٱسْمَ ٱللَّهِ عَلَىٰ مَا رَزَقَهُم مِّنۢ بَهِيمَةِ

ٱلْأَنْعَٰمِ ۗ فَإِلَٰهُكُمْ إِلَٰهٌ وَٰحِدٌ فَلَهُۥٓ أَسْلِمُوا۟ ۗ وَبَشِّرِ ٱلْمُخْبِتِينَ ۞ ٱلَّذِينَ

17

إِذَا ذُكِرَ ٱللَّهُ وَجِلَتْ قُلُوبُهُمْ وَٱلصَّـٰبِرِينَ عَلَىٰ مَآ أَصَابَهُمْ وَٱلْمُقِيمِى ٱلصَّلَوٰةِ وَمِمَّا رَزَقْنَـٰهُمْ يُنفِقُونَ ﴿٣٥﴾

"...and give thou (O beloved Messenger ﷺ) the good news to those who humble themselves. To those whose hearts when Allāh is mentioned, are filled with awe, who show patient perseverance over their afflictions, keep up regular prayer, and spend (in charity) out of what we have bestowed upon them."
(22:34-35)

We understand from this verse that the true practicer of remembrance [*dhākir*] is the one who is humble, remains patient, is steadfast on the five prayers, and spends duly and rightly in the Way of Allāh. This verse also denounces and rejects the false claim of those who pretend to be practicers of remembrance [*dhākirīn*] and imitate the Sufis, yet they are negligent of the ritual prayer [*salāh*]. Nay! They deceive no one but themselves, as the ritual prayer [*salāh*] is the essence and the core of the *dhikr*; without the ritual prayer [*salāh*] *dhikr* is incomplete!

The Sufi saints [*awlīyā'*] state that the *dhikr* of Allāh is incredibly burdensome upon the lower self [*nafs*]. When a person persists in performing *dhikr*, his heart is safeguarded from the attack of his *nafs* and Shaytān. A heedless heart is easy prey for Shaytān, who inclines it toward sin that is why one will not see a Muslim performing *dhikr* in a pub or cinema hall. This shows that

18

dhikr indeed eliminates sin and keeps the practice of remembrance [*dhikr*] away from all types of evil.

Among the meritorious actions that a Muslim may perform, it is *dhikr* whose reward is the greatest. For this reason the purpose and objective of ritual prayer [*salāh*] is the remembrance of Allāh Most Pure [*dhikr*]. It is, therefore, the most important and virtuous form of worship ['*ibādah*] as it combines all aspects of *dhikr* in a single act of '*ibādah*. Allāh the Exalted states:

$$ \text{إِنَّنِىٓ أَنَا ٱللَّهُ لَآ إِلَـٰهَ إِلَّآ أَنَا۠ فَٱعْبُدْنِى وَأَقِمِ ٱلصَّلَوٰةَ لِذِكْرِىٓ} \text{۝} $$

"Verily, I am Allāh. There is no god but I: so serve Me (alone), and establish regular prayer for celebrating My praise."
(20:14)

A great gnostic, Sahl ibn 'Abdullāh ﷺ, has said:[8] "For those who sincerely recite *lā ilāha illa'llāh*, there is no reward but the ultimate vision of Allāh, whereas Paradise [*jannah*] is the ultimate reward for all the other actions. Its evidence is the following verse:

$$ \text{فَٱذْكُرُونِىٓ أَذْكُرْكُمْ وَٱشْكُرُوا۟ لِى وَلَا تَكْفُرُونِ} \text{۝} $$

"Then do ye remember Me; I will remember you. Be grateful to me, and reject not faith." (2:152)

---

[8] See *Mafātīh al-Jinān Sharh Shir'ah al-Islām* by 'Alī Zādah.

The remembrance of Allāh is accomplished through two means: One is to remember His Attributes such as His Sublimity, His Supremacy and to mention His Mercy and Forgiveness. The second is to invoke Him that is to supplicate to Him for one's needs. The prayer of supplication [*du'ā*] is also *dhikr*, but whilst mentioning a need. The former is *dhikr* purely for the sake of Allāh Almighty without any mention of one's wants or needs. It can, however, be deduced from this that there is a very subtle difference between *dhikr* and *du'ā*.

In consequence, there is a difference of opinion between the scholars ['*Ulamā*] as to which is more virtuous, the prayer of supplication [*du'ā*] or divine remembrance [*dhikr*]. After a thorough analysis of the evidence for both, it becomes clear that the latter is more virtuous than the former as there is no ulterior motivation behind *dhikr*, whereas the prayer of supplication [*du'ā*] may have another motivation behind it, such as the fulfillment of a want or need that pertains to this world and oneself.

AHĀDĪTH ABOUT THE MERITS OF DHIKR

There are many narrations highlighting the merits and virtues of *dhikr*. Here only a few Ahādīth will be quoted for the sake of brevity.

عن أبى الدرداء ﷺ قال قال رسول الله ﷺ: ألا انبئكم بخير
أعمالكم و أزكاها عند مليككم و أرفعها فى درجاتكم و خير

20

لكم من انفاق الذهب والورق و خير لكم من أن تلقوا عدوكم
فتضربوا أعناقهم و يضربوا أعناقكم؟ قالوا: بلى ـ قال: ذكر الله
[رواه مالك و أحمد و الترمذى وابن ماجه الا أن مالكا وقف
على أبى الدرداء رضى الله عنه]

Abū 'd-Dardā' ﷺ reports that the Messenger of
Allāh ﷺ once asked his Companions: "Shall I tell
you about the best of all deeds, and the best act of
piety in the eyes of your Lord, which will elevate
your status in the hereafter, and is more virtuous
than the spending of gold and silver in the service
of Allāh, or taking part in jihād and slaying or being
slain in the path of Allāh?" He ﷺ answered by
saying: "The *dhikr* of Allāh." (Related by Imām
Mālik ﷺ in his *Muwatta'*, Imām Ahmad ﷺ, at-
Tirmidhī ﷺ, Ibn Mājah, al-Hākim, and al-Bayhaqī
ﷺ. Al-Hākim ﷺ and others declared it *sahīh*.)

Similarly 'Abdullāh ibn Busr ﷺ narrates that a Bedouin
came to the Messenger of Allāh ﷺ and asked:

أى الناس خير؟ فقال: طوبى لمن طال عمره و حسن عمله ـ قال:
يا رسول الله، أى الأعمال أفضل؟ قال: أن تفارق الدنيا و لسانك
رطب من ذكر الله [رواه أحمد والترمذى]

"Who are the best from amongst the people?" The
Messenger of Allāh ﷺ replied, "The one who lives
long and his actions are righteous" He then asked the
Prophet ﷺ: "What is the most virtuous of all deeds?"
The Messenger of Allāh ﷺ replied: "That you depart
from the world in such a state that your tongue is

fresh with the remembrance of Allāh." (Related by Imām Ahmad ❀ and at-Tirmidhī ❀.)

This is the virtue of *dhikr* in general. The prayer of supplication [*du'ā*] is also a form of *dhikr*, in that, the supplicant remembers His Lord by calling upon Him, and then supplicates to Him regarding his needs. Thus, the prayer of supplication [*du'ā*] comprises of both *dhikr* and asking for one's needs to be fulfilled. *Dhikr* comprises solely of the remembrance of Allāh alone and nothing else. On the one hand, *dhikr* is more virtuous than the prayer of supplication [*du'ā*]. On the other hand, if one considers the proofs and arguments for *du'ā*, then it becomes evident that the prayer of supplication [*du'ā*] has greater merit than *dhikr*. The former has been classified as worship, in fact "the essence of worship," because *du'ā* is a combination of two righteous actions: (1) *dhikr*, and (2) sincere supplication [*du'ā*].[9] However, it should be borne in mind that the recitation of the Holy Qur'ān is more virtuous than both *dhikr* and *du'ā*. There is a Hadīth narrated on the authority of Abū Sa'īd al-Khudrī ❀ that testifies to this fact. Allāh's Messenger ❀ has said:

من شغله القرآن عن ذكرى و مسئلتى أعطيته أفضل ما أعطى
السائلين و فضل كلام الله على سائر الكلام كفضل الله على خلقه
[رواه الترمذى والدارمى والبيهقى]

---

[9] Our Prophet ❀ said, "Supplication [*du'ā*] is the essence of worship."(Related by al-Bukhārī.)

"Allāh says: 'Whosoever is preoccupied with the Qur'ān from My remembrance and from supplicating Me, I shall give him better than what I give to the supplicants.' The superiority of Allāh's Speech over all other speech is like the superiority of Allāh over His creation." (Related by at-Tirmidhī ⁂, ad-Dārimī ⁂, al-Bayhaqī ⁂, and Mullā 'Alī al-Qārī in his *Fayd al-Mu'īn 'alā Jam'il-Arba'īn fī Fadl al-Qur'ān al-Mubīn*.)

The aforementioned Hadīth affirms beautifully that the recitation of the Holy Qur'ān holds greater virtue and excellence than any other type of *dhikr*. Not only is the Holy Qur'ān *dhikr* itself, but it is also a prayer of supplication [*du'ā*] and a way of expressing one's needs. As much as possible one should engage himself in the recitation of Allāh's Speech, and thereafter engage in other forms of *dhikr*. Then he should perform the prayer of supplication [*du'ā*] as Allāh is displeased with those who do not supplicate. It is a clear sign of heedlessness, pride and independence on the part of the would-be devotee. It pleases Allāh Most High to see His slaves supplicate to Him, since this is a sign of their devotion, sincerity, and submission to Him.

Once a question was posed to A'lāhadrat Imām Ahmad Ridā Khān ⁂ about a necessary obligation [*wājib*] to which he explained the similarity between *dhikr* and *du'ā*. The questioner wanted to know if the *wājib* would be fulfilled if he recited Sūrah al-Ikhlās instead of *Du'ā al-Qunut* in the Witr prayer. A'lāhadrat replied: "It is apparent that the *wājib* will be accomplished as this is praise [*thanā*] and all praise is *du'ā.*" Then he elaborated on this point further by saying: "In fact, Mullā 'Alī al-Qārī and other great scholars state that every supplication [*du'ā*] is remembrance [*dhikr*] and every remembrance [*dhikr*] is a form of supplication [*du'ā*]. The Messenger ﷺ has stated: 'The most virtuous supplication [*du'ā*] is saying *Alhamdulillāh* (all praise be to God).'" (Narrated by at-Tirmidhī ؓ who graded it as fair. Also related by an-Nasā'ī ؓ, Ibn Mājah ؓ, Ibn Hibbān ؓ, and al-Hākim ؓ from Jābir ibn 'Abdullāh ؓ.)

In reality *dhikr* and *du'ā* share the same ruling, the difference that has been mentioned is quite subtle. For this reason, one will find that books on *du'ā* contain authentic formulae used for the remembrance of Allāh Most Pure [*adhkār*], as well as prayers of supplication. Imām Ahmad Ridā Khān's *al-Wazīfat al-Karīmah* is an example of this. The reader is encouraged to spread *al-Wazīfat al-Karīmah* far and wide. Its litanies and supplications should be memorized and recited in assemblies. Children and other family members should be encouraged to read it on a day-to-day basis so that everyone may reap its blessings and benefits. Since we are living in incredibly difficult times, it becomes even more imperative that we memorize these *du'ās* and make them part of our daily litanies [*wird*], especially in the morning and the evening. This book will also be of tremendous use to us whilst travelling. Seekers should strive to continuously recite the supplications mentioned herein and gain the blessings of both worlds.

24

THE EXCELLENCE AND VIRTUE OF DU'Ā

Some people are reluctant to humble themselves in the court of Allāh Most High, while there are others who constantly turn to their Creator. The former tend to supplicate when afflicted with a difficulty or hardship. They do not remember Allāh before their affliction, nor does this remembrance linger after their difficulty is removed by the bounty of Allāh the Exalted. The Holy Qur'ān declares such ingrates "transgressors":

وَإِذَا مَسَّ ٱلْإِنسَٰنَ ٱلضُّرُّ دَعَانَا لِجَنبِهِۦٓ أَوْ قَاعِدًا أَوْ قَآئِمًا فَلَمَّا كَشَفْنَا عَنْهُ ضُرَّهُۥ مَرَّ كَأَن لَّمْ يَدْعُنَآ إِلَىٰ ضُرٍّ مَّسَّهُۥ ۚ كَذَٰلِكَ زُيِّنَ لِلْمُسْرِفِينَ مَا كَانُوا۟ يَعْمَلُونَ ۝

"When trouble toucheth a man, he crieth unto Us (in all postures) lying down on His side, or sitting, or standing. But when We have solved his trouble, he passeth on his way as if he had never cried to Us for a trouble that touched him! Thus do the deeds of transgressors seem fair in their eyes." (10:12)

There are some who supplicate at times of ease and happiness, but this supplication and humility in Allāh's court intensifies during periods of hardship and need. Then there are some who specifically supplicate for the fulfillment of their wishes and desires. And finally, some people are content with *dhikr*, reciting *tahlīl*,[10] *tasbīh*,[11] and *tahmīd*[12] during the times when Allāh Most High showers His Mercy or when a calamity befalls them. By doing this, each and every problem, every type of distress is eradicated. If in the event that the answer to their supplications is suspended, they remain patient and have complete reliance upon Allāh Most High and remain pleased with what Allāh has decreed for them in hope and aspiration that there is goodness in store for them. This is the state of the common folk [*ām*].

As for the elite servants [*khās*] who have attained perfection, there are some who entrust all of their affairs to Allāh Most High. They remain silent in times of duress, because of their absolute trust in Allāh. However, these are the chosen servants whose every waking moment is in complete conformity with the Sacred Law [*Sharī'ah*]. Their sole intention is to follow in the footsteps of the Beloved ﷺ. Hence, they never exceed the limits or boundaries set by the *Sharī'ah*, not even by an inch. Allāh has given glad-tidings to these fortunate servants for whom He shall give more than what He gives to those who supplicate unto Him.

Those who do not supplicate in His court due to pride, arrogance, heedlessness and their preoccupation with the luxuries of this mundane world are awaiting a self-inflicted punishment from the Most Just of all judges. Such

---

[10] *Tahlīl*: To say, "There is no god, but God [*lā ilāha illa'llāh*]."
[11] *Tasbīh*: To say, "Transcendent is God [*Subhān Allāh*]!"
[12] *Tahmīd*: To say, "All praise belongs to God [*Alhamdulillāh*]."

people have been reprimanded in a Hadīth narrated on the authority of Abū Hurayrah ﷺ:

من لم يسأل الله يغضب عليه

"Whosoever does not supplicate unto Allāh, Allāh is angry with him." (Related by at-Tirmidhī ﷺ.)

Sadly these wretched people will wallow in pits of darkness on account of their egos [*nufūs*], pride, and arrogance. They prefer the life of this world and turn away willfully from Allāh Most Pure. Assuredly, Allāh detests those who are arrogant.

CONCLUSIONS

The prayer of supplication is an unfathomable treasure-trove that contains many blessings and benefits. It is from the wondrous blessings that have been bestowed by the Master to His slaves. Our bountiful Lord has commanded us to raise our hands in supplication to Him:

وَقَالَ رَبُّكُمُ ٱدْعُونِىٓ أَسْتَجِبْ لَكُمْ إِنَّ ٱلَّذِينَ يَسْتَكْبِرُونَ عَنْ عِبَادَتِى سَيَدْخُلُونَ جَهَنَّمَ دَاخِرِينَ ۞

"And your Lord says: 'Call unto Me; and I shall answer your prayer. But those who are too arrogant to worship Me will surely find themselves in Hell in utter humiliation." (40:60)

The Knowers of Intimate Discourse [*munājat*] have tasted fully the sweetness of supplication. Their heads are bowed reverentially in gratitude knowing what an honor it is to raise their hands and call unto Him. Glory be to Allāh [*Subhān Allāh*]!

The Sublime Lord is inviting us to His exalted court, which is an undeserved honor, and He has promised to reward His faithful devotees with eternal blessings. The courts of this world do not even let the visitor tarry beyond their appointed time, let alone answering their needs, fulfilling their desires, or offering them lasting solace. Visitors are quickly dispelled from worldly courts with little more than token favors.

How generous and merciful is the Lord of the worlds, Who is the King of all kings, the Master of all masters! Not only is the prince and the pauper, the young and the old permitted to enter His esteemed court, He even invites them to call unto Him, to supplicate to Him, to present their needs to Him. Tragically some flee from Allāh, the Sublime and Exalted, and deprive themselves of His benevolence and infinite mercy.

Therefore to present oneself in His noble court, to sincerely supplicate unto Him and surrender one's needs before Him, is the key that opens the door to His Mercy. The prayer of supplication is a believer's most powerful weapon. It is one of the few acts of worship that can alter one's destiny. It is the "essence" of worship and the pinnacle of obedience to Allāh Almighty. With it we can never fail; without it we can never succeed. The question of *du'ā* is incredibly pertinent in light of the suffering and calamities, which have confronted the Community of Sayyidunā Muhammad ﷺ in various parts of the world today. With the Hour being near, *du'ā* should not be marginalized or ridiculed. And yet it has almost become a forgotten aspect of Islamic worship, partially because our notions about the importance of supplication have become distorted and (in some instances) challenged by misguided groups. Often it is reduced to a mere ritual, or it is belittled through careless actions and sometimes even with unworthy speech.

Du'ā is conversation with Allāh, our Creator, our Cherisher, our Lord and Master, the All-Knowing, the All-Powerful, the Responsive One Who answers those who beseech Him. The act of *du'ā* is not only empowering, but also enables us to actively converse with the Source of Peace.[13] We turn to Him because we know that He will certainly listen to us. Hence, we experience a sense of relief and spiritual elation after worship ['*ibādah*]. A person who engages in *du'ā* understands and cherishes his relationship with the Creator of all things! He seeks to constantly fortify this precious bond through constant remembrance [*dhikr*] and sincere supplication [*du'ā*].

Sadly atrocities are commonplace today in the lands of Islam. As a Community we are experiencing everything

---

[13] *Yā Salām* [O Source of Peace!] is one of the ninety-nine Names of Allāh as mentioned in Sūrah 59, al-Hashr ["The Mustering"].

from unholy wars to natural disasters like floods, earthquakes, and even Tsunamis. Suicide-bombers have violated the pure *Sharī'ah* by hijacking our religion and killing innocent civilians. In 2010, suicide-bombers desolated the blessed mausoleums of celebrated Sufi saints [*awliyā'*] including, the famous shrine in Pakistan's Punjab province that is the resting place of Hadrat Bābā Farid ad-Dīn Ganj-e Shakar ؓ, as well as Dāta Darbar in the eastern Pakistanī city of Lahore, which is the resting place of Shaykh 'Alī ibn 'Uthmān "Dāta 'Alī al-Hijwarī" ؓ. On April 11, 2011 suicide-attackers martyred at least forty-one people and wounded many more near the Sakhi Sarwar shrine in Punjab, which is the resting place of Hadrat 'Abdullāh Shāh Ghazī ؓ.

These malicious attacks on the blessed mausoleums of the *awliyā'* were followed by political unrest in Egypt, Libya, and Syria. There is still unrest in all of these nations despite countless diplomatic efforts to restore peace and normalcy. Militant groups are exploiting the situation and have attacked about a half-dozen mausoleums in and around Tripoli, Libya. Hard-liners, who desecrate graves in the name of "Islamic" reform and revolution, are vandals and fanatics that know little to nothing about traditional, mainstream Islam.[14] It is true that the old

---

[14] Imām Ahmad Ridā Khān ؓ wrote a significant tract against desecrating mausoleums, titled *Ihlāk-ul-Wahābiyyīn 'alā Tawhīn Qubūr il Muslimīn* [Chastising the Wahhābīs for Disrespecting the Graves of Muslims]. It admonishes Muslims to follow the Sunnah of Sayyidunā Muhammad ﷺ and forsake the pernicious ideology of Muhammad ibn 'Abd al-Wahhāb (d. 1206/1792) and Ismā'īl ad-Dihlawī (d. 1246/1831).

draconian regimes in these countries had needlessly stained their hands with the blood of innocent civilians, and crushed the spirit of their own people. But it is also true that chaos is worse than tyranny and the new vanguard, ready for battle, may be even worse than their former despots. One cannot underestimate the pain that the Muslim *ummah* is feeling for the beautiful people of Egypt, Libya, and Syria. The question arises as to how we should respond. Should we become apathetic or politically active by signing petitions and participating in peaceful demonstrations? Then again, what is the long-term efficacy of such short-lived efforts, especially when today's news will be lining tomorrow's trashcans? How quickly we forget someone else's pain, and move on to something else. Our tendency is to be active today and indifferent tomorrow.

The most powerful tool within the believers' arsenal in these horrendous times is sincere supplication. A Muslim in the United Kingdom praying for his brothers and sisters in Egypt, Libya, and Syria may through the grace of Allāh, the Exalted, save someone from a terrible calamity. If forty Muslims get together to make *dhikr* in America and then transfer the merit of this virtuous deed [*isal al-thawab*] to our brethren in the lands of Islam, Allāh Most High may accept our intention and bless those people and ease their difficulties. This is what we fail to understand today. We look only to this physical world for answers to our problems, and forget to believe in the unseen [*ghayb*].

A true Muslim will always turn to his Creator, Sustainer, and Protector whenever obstacles come in his way, because he knows that *Allāhu Akbar* (God is the Greatest)! We turn to Him through *dhikr* and *du'ā*, which fills our hearts with love, joy, peace, patience, gentleness, and fortitude. Our Lord is the Most Merciful of those who show mercy; and He is nearer to us than our jugular vein:

وَلَقَدْ خَلَقْنَا ٱلْإِنسَٰنَ وَنَعْلَمُ مَا تُوَسْوِسُ بِهِۦ نَفْسُهُۥ ۖ وَنَحْنُ أَقْرَبُ إِلَيْهِ

مِنْ حَبْلِ ٱلْوَرِيدِ ﴿١٦﴾

"It is We who created man, and We know what dark suggestions his soul makes to him: for We are nearer to him than (his) jugular vein." (50:16)

وَإِذَا سَأَلَكَ عِبَادِى عَنِّى فَإِنِّى قَرِيبٌ ۖ أُجِيبُ دَعْوَةَ ٱلدَّاعِ إِذَا دَعَانِ

فَلْيَسْتَجِيبُوا۟ لِى وَلْيُؤْمِنُوا۟ بِى لَعَلَّهُمْ يَرْشُدُونَ ﴿١٨٦﴾

"When My servants ask thee concerning Me, I am indeed close (to them): I listen to the prayer of every suppliant when He calleth on Me: let them also, with a will, listen to My call, and believe in Me: that they may walk in the right way." (2:186)

Assuredly, it is only Allāh Who is the remover of difficulties, Who is the eradicator of all problems, and Who answers the prayer of the oppressed:

أَمَّن يُجِيبُ ٱلْمُضْطَرَّ إِذَا دَعَاهُ وَيَكْشِفُ ٱلسُّوٓءَ وَيَجْعَلُكُمْ خُلَفَآءَ
ٱلْأَرْضِ ۗ أَءِلَهٌ مَّعَ ٱللَّهِ ۚ قَلِيلًا مَّا تَذَكَّرُونَ ۞

*"Or, who listens to the (soul) distressed when it calls on Him,
and who relieves its suffering, and makes you (mankind)
inheritors of the earth? (Can there be another) god besides
Allāh. Little it is that ye heed!"* (27: 62)

Since *dhikr* is also a form of *du'ā*, we will now relate a few
essential etiquettes [*ādāb*] that one should adhere to before
and after making *du'ā* so that we might fully reap the fruits
our supplication. The esteemed father of A'lāhadrat Imām
Ahmad Ridā Khān al-Qādirī ﷺ, *'Umdat al-Muhaqqiqīn*[15]
Sanad al-'Arifīn[16] Shaykh Naqī 'Alī Khān al-Barakātī ﷺ, has
compiled an excellent book on the benefits, virtues and
excellence of *du'ā* with the name *Ahsan al-Wi'a li-Ādāb ad-
Du'ā* [The Perfect Vase for Gathering the Etiquettes of
Supplication]. Imām Ahmad Ridā Khān ﷺ wrote a
commentary to this book entitled, *Dhayl al-Mudda'a li-
Ahsan al-Wi'a* [A Supplement to the Perfect Vase]. The
following points were excerpted from this masterpiece for
the benefit of the reader:

- When making *du'ā* empty the heart of all other
  thoughts as much as humanly possible.

---

[15] The Pillar of the Research-Scholars
[16] The Support of the Gnostics

- The body, clothes, and place of *du'ā* must be pure and clean.

- Try and perform a virtuous deed prior to making *du'ā* [e.g., give something in charity].

- If there are any rights binding on the supplicant, then these should be fulfilled, or pardoned (if possible) from the owner(s) of these rights.

- Always abstain from consumption of unlawful food and drinks. Do not wear clothing that is bought from unlawful money, as the supplication of negligent people, who indulge in unlawful matters, will be rejected.

- Repent from all previous sins before making *du'ā*.

- If the time is not disliked [*makrūh*], then perform two cycles [*raka'āt*] of ritual prayer [*salāh*] prior to making *du'ā*. This attracts the mercy of Allāh.

- Try to be in a state of ritual purity [*wudū'*], facing the *Qibla*, and sit in the *Qā'idah* (or sitting) position for prayer, or the kneeling posture.

- Alert the organs of the physical body to be fearful of Allāh Almighty, and condition the heart to be attentive and present.

- Always lower your gaze, and be sure not to look at that which is unlawful.

- Always glorify Allāh and praise Him at the beginning and at the end.

- Before commencing the praise [*hamd*] of Allāh and the prayer of supplication [*du'ā*] itself, always recite prayers on the beloved Messenger 鷺, his noble Family and illustrious Companions [*salawāt*], and be sure to close your supplication with *salawāt*.

- When making *du'ā* concentrate on Allāh's divine majesty and status.

- Always be grateful to Allāh for the abundant blessings that He bestows upon us, and recognize how shamelessly we behave toward Him, despite His infinite generosity, by sinning and disobeying His commandments.

- Pay special attention to the power of Allāh and our state of inferiority and our total dependence on Him.

- Use the Splendid Names of Allāh [*al-Asmā' al-'Izām*] when beginning the prayer of supplication. For instance, *Yā Arhamar Rāhimīn* [O the Most Merciful of those who show mercy], or *Yā Rabbanā* [O our Lord, our Sustainer] five times.

- Seek a means [*tawassul*][17] when making *du'ā* by giving special emphasis to the Splendid Names and Divine Attributes of Allāh, His Books especially the Mother of All Books (the Holy Qur'ān), His Prophets and Angels, the Master of the Messengers ﷺ, the Friends of Allāh in general, and the Chieftain of the Saints, Sultan al-Awliyā,

---

[17] *Tawassul*: To supplicate to Allāh through an intermediary, such as saying, "O Allāh! I ask you by the rank of Your Prophet ﷺ." It is also permissible to perform *tawassul* through a living person, a dead person, a good deed, the personal relics of the Prophets and Sufi saints, or a Name or Attribute of Allāh Most High.

al-Ghawth al-A'zam Sayyidunā ash-Shaykh Muhyid'dīn 'Abd al-Qādir al-Jīlānī ﷺ in particular.

- Also present those deeds performed solely for His sake as a means [*tawassul*].
- Being conscious of the One, with Whom you speak, raise your hands parallel to the chest, or the shoulder, or face, or raise them higher still with utmost etiquette [*ādāb*].
- The palms must be side-by-side, opened flat facing skywards.
- Adopt a soft tone when making *du'ā*.
- Try to make *du'ā* in private.
- Always exercise humility and weep whilst making *du'ā*.
- There must be fervent repetition and persistence in making *du'ā*.
- *Du'ā* must be made with surety and full determination.

Once a person adheres to these etiquettes and fulfills the conditions which are pivotal to the acceptance of his *du'ās*, then he will reap the harvest of his efforts.

May Allāh the Exalted grant us the enabling grace [*tawfīq*] to cleanse ourselves inwardly and outwardly and may He grant us the *tawfīq* to invoke Him in every moment of our lives and may we be among those who sincerely repentant, those who are pure, and those who are from His righteous servants, āmīn.

لَا يُكَلِّفُ ٱللَّهُ نَفْسًا إِلَّا وُسْعَهَا ۚ لَهَا مَا كَسَبَتْ وَعَلَيْهَا مَا ٱكْتَسَبَتْ ۗ رَبَّنَا لَا

تُؤَاخِذْنَا إِن نَّسِينَا أَوْ أَخْطَأْنَا ۚ رَبَّنَا وَلَا تَحْمِلْ عَلَيْنَا إِصْرًا كَمَا حَمَلْتَهُ عَلَى

ٱلَّذِينَ مِن قَبْلِنَا ۚ رَبَّنَا وَلَا تُحَمِّلْنَا مَا لَا طَاقَةَ لَنَا بِهِ ۖ وَٱعْفُ عَنَّا وَٱغْفِرْ لَنَا

وَٱرْحَمْنَا ۚ أَنتَ مَوْلَىٰنَا فَٱنصُرْنَا عَلَى ٱلْقَوْمِ ٱلْكَـٰفِرِينَ ﴿٢٨٦﴾

*"On no soul doth Allāh place a burden greater than it can
bear. It gets every good that it earns, and it suffers every ill
that it earns. (Pray:) 'Our Lord! Condemn us not if we forget
or fall into error. Our Lord! Lay not on us a burden like that
which Thou didst lay on those before us. Our Lord! Lay not on
us a burden greater than we have strength to bear. Blot out
our sins, and grant us forgiveness have mercy on us. Thou art
our Protector; help us against those who stand against faith.'"*
(2:286)

Author's Supplication

[Imām Ahmad Ridā Khān ﷺ begins the present work with a sermon, or *khutbah*, comprising of an invocation in the Arabic language. The original Arabic text is presented here along with its English translation. It is followed by Hujjat al-Islām Shaykh Hāmid Ridā Khān's "Prologue."]

بسم الله الرحمن الرحيم

حامدا لمن جعل الدعاء عبادة بل مخ العبادة و أمر بأدعونى عباده وألزمه بوعده الإجابة و من دعا ربه لبيك يا عبدى أجابه قال ربكم أدعونى أستجب لكم و أذا سألك عبادى عنى فانى قريب أجيب دعوة الداع إذا دعان فإنه سميع مجيب و مصليا و مسلما على من اختبا دعوته المستجابة ليوم المثابة و على آله و أصحابه ما انهل الديم من السحابة ـ آمين

In the Name of Allāh,
the Most Gracious, the Most Merciful

I praise the One, Who has made supplication [*du'ā*] an act of worship—nay, the essence of worship. And He has given His servants a positive command with the words *Supplicate unto Me*, and He has vouchsafed the acceptance of our prayers. Whosoever calls upon His Lord, He

38

answers: O My slave, I am here! *And your Lord says: "Call on Me; and I will answer your prayer. Verily, those who are too proud to worship Me will enter Hell despised."*[18] *And (O beloved Messenger* 🌸*) when My servants ask you concerning Me, then surely I am near; I answer the call of the supplicant when he calls unto Me;*[19] He is indeed the All-Hearing, the One, Who accepts and answers prayers.

I send blessings and salutations upon the one who reserved his accepted supplication for the Day of Assembly [*qiyāmah*] 🌸 and upon his noble Family and his illustrious Companions as long as the rain continues to pour forth from the sky. O Lord, accept [this prayer]!

---

[18] Sūrah al-Ghāfir, 40:60.
[19] Sūrah al-Baqarah, 2:186.

Prologue
By Shaykh Hāmid Ridā Khān 🌸

A'lāhadrat Imām Ahmad Ridā Khān 🌸 desired to write a few introductory words to this book, but these remained concealed with him like hidden pearls. It was only after his union [*wisāl*] with Allāh Most Pure in 1340/1921 that these precious words were discovered amongst the relics in our family home. I did not want a single letter to be altered or removed from the original Arabic text penned by A'lāhadrat 🌸 in his characteristic style. Consequentially, this text has been faithfully recorded word for word in the chapter entitled, "Author's Supplication," and hereby presented to the beloved readers. A title for this work was also not given, thus the historical name and the introductory sermon [*khutbah*] were added by this humble beggar [*faqīr*] of the Real (Allāh the Exalted).

All praise belongs to Allāh Most High, Who made us servants in the noble court of the Master of the World, Sayyidunā Muhammad,[20] the Messenger of Allāh 🌸; and placed in our hands the robe of mercy of the Mightiest Succor [*al-Ghawth al-A'zam*], Sayyidunā ash-Shaykh Muhyid'dīn 'Abd al-Qādir al-Jīlānī al-Baghdādī al-Hasanī

---

[20] *Sayyidunā*: "Our Master."

al-Husaynī ﷺ; and increased the life of the *Mashāyikh* of our spiritual order, especially Sayyidunā A'lāhadrat Imām Ahmad Ridā Khān ﷺ, who handed-down to us the saying, "your Lord is not shy [*hayā*],"[21] which means He will not shy away from the one who turns to Him through sincere supplication and leave him empty-handed. Allāh the Exalted has Himself commanded us to invoke Him and present our humble supplications to Him, and He has made the acceptance of such prayers and invocations necessary upon His esteemed Being.

فعليكم بالدعاء فإن الدعاء يرد القضاء بعد أن يبرم

"So hold fast to supplication [*du'ā*] for indeed it is *du'ā* that averts fate, [even] after it has been commenced." (Ibn Mājah has related a Hadīth

---

[21] Our Prophet ﷺ has said, "Indeed, Allāh is Shy and Beneficent. He is shy when His servant raises his hands to Him (in supplication) to return them empty, disappointed!" (Narrated by Imām Ahmad ﷺ, Abū Dāwūd ﷺ, and at-Tirmidhī ﷺ.) Muslims must not interpret these words literally to mean "diffident, timid, cautious or reluctant," because Allāh Most Pure is free from feelings and emotions, which are created and thus contingent [*hādith*], originated and finite. The People of the Prophetic Way and the Majority of Scholars affirm that Allāh and His Attributes are preexistent without origin and eternal without end [*qadīm*]. The Arabic word *hayā* (or, "shy") that appears in this Hadīth Sharīf is linguistically unclear [*mutashābihāt*], and should be interpreted allegorically. Its actual meaning will not contradict the categorical Qur'ānic verse: *Naught is as His likeness* (42:11).

similar to this one with the wording: "Nothing
increases a person's life span except goodly actions,
and nothing averts fate except supplication.")

The book you are holding contains authoritative
supplications [*du'ās*] and litanies [*wazā'if*] that were
preserved like secret treasures within the Lofty Household
of Saints [*Khandan-e-'Āliyah*] and transmitted to us from
the noble Messenger of Allāh 🌸 through our mentor,
Sayyidunā A'lāhadrat Imām Ahmad Ridā Khān ⚅. We
(the compilers of this work) declare that anyone who
sincerely acts upon the prayers within this book and
recites them regularly shall be blessed with the blessings of
both worlds, and he will be safeguarded from all
calamities within and without.

May Allāh Most High grant blessings to the People of
the Prophetic Way and the Majority of Scholars [*Ahl al-
Sunnah wa al-Jamā'ah*] through the blessings of these
prayers and supplications, āmīn.

—Muhammad Hāmid Ridā Khān al-Qādirī ⚅
A *faqīr* in the noble Court of Ridā

Supplications upon Waking

Upon waking the supplicant should read this *du'ā*, which will enable him to rise on the Day of Judgment [*qiyāmah*] whilst making the *dhikr* of Allāh Almighty.[22]

اَلْحَمْدُ لِلّٰهِ الَّذِىْ اَحْيَانَا بَعْدَ مَا اَمَاتَنَا وَ اِلَيْهِ النُّشُوْرُ

Alhamdulillāhil ladhī ahyānā ba'da mā amātanā wa ilayhin nushūr.

"All praise belongs to Allāh, Who has granted us life after death[23] and towards Him shall we be gathered on the Day of Resurrection."

---

[22] Related by Imām an-Nawawī in his *al-Adhkār*, p. 26 (#39). Also narrated on the authority of Hudhayfa ﷺ in *Saḥīḥ al-Bukhārī* (#6312, 6314, 6324, 7394); *Jāmi' al-Tirmidhī* (#3413); *Sunan Abū Dāwūd* (#5049); *Musnad Aḥmad* vol. 5/pp. 385, 387, 397, 399, 407; *Sunan Ibn Mājah* (#3880); by ad-Dārimī in his *Sunan* (#2689); and by an-Nasā'ī in *'Amal al-Yawm wa'l Laylah* (#737-749, 856-860). It is also related on the authority of Abū Dharr ﷺ in *Saḥīḥ al-Bukhārī* (#6325, 7395) and an-Nasā'ī in *'Amal al-Yawm wa'l Laylah* (#750, 860).
[23] It is said that sleep is the twin brother of death.

It is important to remember that before and after every litany, the supplicant must send blessings and salutations upon the Chosen One ﷺ [*durūd sharīf*] either once, thrice, or eleven times. This will ensure that his litany is accepted in the court of Allāh Almighty.[24]

<hr>

[24] At-Tirmidhī narrated that 'Umar bin al-Khattāb ؓ said: "A supplication remains suspended between heaven and earth and does not ascend any further until you send salutations upon your Prophet." Razin ibn Mu'awiyah ؓ in his book *Jāmi' al-Usūl* reported this Hadīth Sharīf from the Messenger of Allāh ﷺ with the words: "A supplication remains suspended between heaven and earth and does not ascend any further until a person sends salutations upon me... send salutations upon me at the beginning of your supplication, at the end, and in the middle." The Prophet ﷺ is central and he is reminding us of his centrality, as the Key of Mercy, the Key of Paradise, and the Chosen One with whom Allāh is well pleased. The Exalted says to the faithful in Sūrah al-Ahzāb: *Verily Allāh and His angels whelm the Prophet in blessings. O ye who believe, invoke blessings upon him, and give him greetings of peace* (33:56).

Supplications after the Ritual Prayer

(1) Recite the Verse of the Throne [*Āyat al-Kursī*]²⁵ once.²⁶

ٱللَّهُ لَآ إِلَهَ إِلَّا هُوَ ٱلْحَيُّ ٱلْقَيُّومُ ۚ لَا تَأْخُذُهُ سِنَةٌ وَلَا نَوْمٌ ۚ لَّهُ مَا

فِى ٱلسَّمَٰوَٰتِ وَمَا فِى ٱلْأَرْضِ ۗ مَن ذَا ٱلَّذِى يَشْفَعُ عِندَهُۥ إِلَّا

بِإِذْنِهِ ۚ يَعْلَمُ مَا بَيْنَ أَيْدِيهِمْ وَمَا خَلْفَهُمْ ۖ وَلَا يُحِيطُونَ بِشَىْءٍ

مِّنْ عِلْمِهِۦٓ إِلَّا بِمَا شَآءَ ۚ وَسِعَ كُرْسِيُّهُ ٱلسَّمَٰوَٰتِ وَٱلْأَرْضَ ۖ وَلَا

يَـُٔودُهُۥ حِفْظُهُمَا ۚ وَهُوَ ٱلْعَلِىُّ ٱلْعَظِيمُ ﴿٢٥٥﴾

Allāhu lā ilāha 'illā huwa'l-Hayyul-Qayyūm. Lā ta'-khuzuhū sina-tunw-wa lā nawm. Lahū mā fissamāwāti wa mā fil-'ard. Man-Dhālladhī yashfa-'u 'indahū illā bī-idhnih. Ya-'lamu mā bayna aydīhim wa mā khalfahum. Wa lā yu-hītūna bi-shay-'im min 'il-mihī 'illā bimā shā'. Wa-si-'a

---

²⁵ Sūrah al-Baqarah, 2:255.
²⁶ *Tadhkirat al-Muttaqīn*, vol. 1/p. 129; at-Tabarānī in his *al-Mu'jam al-Kabīr; Mishkāt al-Masābīh*, vol. 1/p. 89.

Kursiyyu-hus-Samāwā-ti wāl-'ard; wa lā ya-'ūdu-
hu hifzu-humā wa Huwal-'Aliyyul-'Azīm.

Allāh, there is no god but He, the Living, the
Everlasting. Slumber seizes Him not, neither sleep;
to Him belongs all that is in the heavens and the
earth. Who is there that shall intercede with Him
save by His leave? He knows what lies before them
and what is after them, and they comprehend not
anything of His knowledge save such as He wills.
His Throne comprises the heavens and earth; the
preserving of them oppresses Him not; He is the
All-High, the All-Glorious.

(2) Recite the following prayer of forgiveness [*istighfār*]
three times:[27]

اَسْتَغْفِرُ اللّٰهَ الَّذِىْ لاَ اِلٰهَ اِلاَّ هُوَ الْحَىُّ الْقَيُّومُ وَ اَتُوْبُ
اِلَيْه

Astaghfiru 'Llāhal-ladhī lā ilāha illā Huwal Hayyul
Qayyūmu wa atūbu ilayh

I seek forgiveness from Allāh—besides Whom there
is no one worthy of worship—the Living, the Self-
Subsisting, and I turn to Him in repentance.

---

[27] *Sunan Abū Dāwūd* (#1517); *Jāmi' al-Tirmidhī*, vol. 2/p. 177 (#3572); *al-
Targhīb wat Tarhīb*, vol. 2/p. 470; and al-Hākim in his *al-Mustadrak*, vol.
1/p. 511.

(3) Recite the glorification [*tasbīh*] given to Sayyidah Fatima ﴾ by the Messenger of Allāh ﷺ: Say, "Subhān Allāh" thirty-three times, "Alhamdulillāh" thirty-three times, and "Allāhu Akbar" thirty-four times.[28] Upon completing this *tasbīh* the supplicant should recite:[29]

$$\text{لَا إِلٰهَ إِلَّا اللهُ وَحْدَهُ لَا شَرِيْكَ لَهُ لَهُ الْمُلْكُ وَ لَهُ}$$
$$\text{الْحَمْدُ وَ هُوَ عَلٰى كُلِّ شَيْءٍ قَدِيْرٌ}$$

Lā ilāha illa Allāhu Wahdahu lā sharīka lah. Lahul Mulku wa lahul Hamdu wa Huwa 'alā kulli shay'in Qadīr.

There is no god but Allāh alone, Who is One without partner. His is the dominion, all praise belongs to Him, and He has power over everything.

(4) After each obligatory ritual prayer [*fard salāh*], the *namāzī*[30] should place his right-hand on his forehead and read:[31]

---

[28] *Sahīh al-Bukhārī*, vol. 2/p. 935 (#3113, 3705, 5361-5362, 6318); *Sahīh Muslim*, vol. 2/p. 351 (#2727); *Sunan Abū Dāwūd*, p. 350 (#5062-5063); *Jāmi' al-Tirmidhī*, vol. 2/p. 178 (#3405, 5062); *Musnad Ahmad*, vol. 1/p. 96; *Musnad al-Dārimī* (#2688).

[29] *Sahīh al-Bukhārī*, vol. 2/p. 947; *Sahīh Muslim*; *Sunan Abū Dāwūd* (#5052); an-Nasā'ī in *'Amal al-Yawm wa'l Laylah* (#767); Ibn al-Sunnī in his *'Amal al-Yawm wa'l Laylah* (#713).

[30] *Namāzī*: a person who is prayerful; devout.

[31] *Al-Hisn al-Hasīn*, p. 105; *al-Adhkār al-Muntakhaba min Kalām Sayyid al-Abrār* by Imām an-Nawawī.

بِسْمِ اللهِ الَّذِىْ لَا اِلٰهَ اِلَّا هُوَ الرَّحْمٰنُ الرَّحِيْمُ.اَللّٰهُمَّ اَذْهِبْ عَنِّى الْهَمَّ وَالْحُزْنَ

Bismil lāhil ladhī lā ilāha illā Huwar Rahmānur Rahīm. Allāhumma Adh-hib 'annil hamma wal huzn.

In the Name of Allāh, there is no one worthy of worship except Him, the Most Affectionate, the Ever-Merciful. O Allāh, remove anxiety and sorrow from me.

Supplications after the Fajr Prayer

(1) This *du'ā* protects the supplicant from Shaytān, the accursed, and all his undertakings become easy; his anxiety is removed, his faith [*īmān*] is safeguarded, his enemy will self-destruct, his good deeds will increase, and it will become easy for him to walk across the Bridge over the fire. It should be read once or three times:[32]

---

[32] Buraydah ❀ relates that the Messenger of Allāh ﷺ said: "The one who recites the following ten phrases after his ritual prayer shall find Allāh sufficient for five of his worldly objectives and five of his affairs related to the hereafter, *(1) Hasbiy Allāhu li-Dīni (2) Hasbiy Allāhu li-Dunyāya (3) Hasbiy Allāhu lima Ahammani (4) Hasbiy Allāhu līmān Bagha 'Alayy (5) Hasbiy Allāhu li-man Hasadani (6) Hasbiya Allāhu li-man Kadani bi-Sū' (7) Hasbiy Allāhu 'indal Mawt (8) Hasbiy Allāhu 'indal Mas'alati fil-Qabr (9) Hasbiy Allāhu 'indal Mizan (10) Hasbiy Allāhu 'indas Sirāt (11) Hasbiy Allāhu lā ilāha illa Huwa 'alayhi tawakkaltu wa ilayhi Unīb"* (*Nawadir al-Usūl fi Ahādīth al-Rasūl* ﷺ, vol. 2/p 163). There is a similar narration in Shaykh 'Abdur Rahman Suhaym's *al-Fatāwā al-'Ammah*, vol. 1/p. 59. This book cites Ma'rūf al-Karkhī ❀, a renowned Sufi saint (d. 200/815) from Baghdad, who offered this supplication frequently in his prayers: "*Hasbiy Allāhu li-Dunyāya Hasbiy Allāhu li-Dīni Hasbiy Allāhu lima Ahammani Hasbiy Allāhul Hakīmul Qawiyy līmān Bagha 'Alayy, Hasbiy Allāhush-Shadīd li-man Kadani bi-Sū' Hasbiy Allāhur Rahīm 'indal Mawt, Hasbiy Allāhur Ra'ūf 'indal Mas'alati fil-Qabr, HasbiyAllāhu 'indal Hisāb, Hasbiy Allāhul-Latif 'indal Mizān HasbiyAllāhul Qadīr 'indas*

اَللّٰهُمَّ اكْفِنِىْ كُلَّ مُهِمٍّ مِّنْ حَيْثُ شِئْتَ وَ مِنْ اَيْنَ شِئْتَ حَسْبِىَ اللّٰهُ لِدِيْنِىْ حَسْبِىَ اللّٰهُ لِدُنْيَاىَ حَسْبِىَ اللّٰهُ لِمَا اَهَمَّنِىْ حَسْبِىَ اللّٰهُ لِمَنْ بَغَى عَلَىَّ حَسْبِىَ اللّٰهُ لِمَنْ حَسَدَنِىْ حَسْبِىَ اللّٰهُ لِمَنْ كَادَنِىْ بِسُوْءٍ حَسْبِىَ اللّٰهُ عِنْدَ الْمَوْتِ حَسْبِىَ اللّٰهُ عِنْدَ الْمَسْئَلَةِ فِى الْقَبْرِ حَسْبِىَ اللّٰهُ عِنْدَ الْمِيْزَانِ حَسْبِىَ اللّٰهُ عِنْدَ الصِّرَاطِ حَسْبِىَ اللّٰهُ الَّذِىْ لَا اِلٰهَ اِلَّا هُوَ عَلَيْهِ تَوَكَّلْتُ وَ هُوَ رَبُّ الْعَرْشِ الْعَظِيْمِ

Allāhummak finī kulla muhimmin min haythu shi'ta wa min ayna shi'ta hasbiy-Allāhu li Dīnī Hasbiy-Allāhu li Dunyāyat hasbiy-Allāhu limā Aham-mani Hasbiy-Allāhu li-man baghā Hasbiy-Allāhu līmān Hasadanī Hasbiy-Allāhu li man kādanī bi sū'in Hasbiy-Allāhu 'indal mawt. Hasbiy-Allāhu 'indal mas'alati fil Qabr. Hasbiy-Allāhu 'indal mīzān. Hasbiy-Allāhu 'indas Sirāt. Hasbiy-Allāhul ladhī lā ilāha illa Huwa 'alayhi tawakkaltu wa Huwa Rabbul 'Arshil 'Azīm.

O Allāh, suffice me in every important affair however You will and from wherever You will. Allāh is sufficient for me for my religion. Allāh is sufficient for me for my worldly affairs. Allāh is

Sirāt, Hasbiy Allāhu lā ilāha illa Huwa 'alayhi tawakkaltu wa Huwa Rabbul 'Arshil 'Azīm."

sufficient for me for whatever troubles me. Allāh is sufficient for me for whosoever trespassed against me. Allāh is sufficient for me for whosoever looked upon me with envy. Allāh is sufficient for me for whosoever plotted evil against me. Allāh is sufficient for me at the time of death. Allāh is sufficient for me at the time of questioning in the grave. Allāh is sufficient for me at the weighing of deeds. Allāh is sufficient for me at the crossing of the Traverse. Allāh is sufficient for me. There is none worthy of worship save Him. I have placed my trust in Him, and He is the Lord of the Majestic Throne.

(2) After the recitation of litanies [wazā'if] is complete, the supplicant should sit and wait till the sun rises. Then he should perform (at least) two cycles [raka'āt] of the mid-morning prayer [Salāh ad-Duhā],[33] which occurs approximately twenty minutes after sunrise. It is narrated that by performing this supererogatory ritual prayer [nafl salāh] a Muslim will attain the reward [thawāb] of a greater Pilgrimage [Hajj] and lesser Pilgrimage [Umrah].

Translator's Commentary: It is worth noting that there is a difference of opinion regarding Salāh al-'Ishrāq and Salāh ad-Duhā. Classical scholars hold the view that the post-sunrise prayer [ishrāq] is the same as of the mid-morning prayer [duhā] like the great Egyptian gnostic and erudite

---

[33] The Duhā prayer is also known as the Chasht prayer among Muslims following the Hanafī school in the Subcontinent.

51

scholar Imām 'Abd al-Wahhāb al-Sha'rānī ﷺ (d. 973/1565) in his *Lawāqih al-Anwār al-Qudsiyyah* [The Enrichment of Sacred Illuminations].[34] Scholars from the Subcontinent, however, mention the two prayers separately. Regardless of the position one takes, the Duhā prayer holds tremendous reward.

The post-sunrise prayer [*Salāh al-Ishrāq*] is offered immediately after sunrise. Anas ibn Mālik ﷺ relates that the Messenger of Allāh ﷺ said: "Whosoever offers the Fajr prayer in congregation, then remains seated making *dhikr* until sunrise, and thereafter offers two cycles [of supererogatory prayer], he shall attain the reward of performing a Hajj and 'Umrah."[35]

Anas ibn Mālik ﷺ also relates the following about the mid-morning prayer [*Salāh ad-Duhā*],[36] which is offered halfway between sunrise and the time of the sun's zenith [*zawāl*]: "I heard the Messenger of Allāh ﷺ say, 'Whosoever recites twelve cycles of *Salāh ad-Duhā*, Allāh shall erect for him a palace of gold in Paradise.'"[37]

According to Imām al-Sha'rānī ﷺ one of the benefits of persisting in the performance of *Salāh ad-Duhā* is that the practitioner will be protected from the influence of Jinn.

---

[34] See *Lawāqih al-Anwār al-Qudsiyyah fī Bayān al-'Uhūd al-Muhammadiyyah*, p. 80.

[35] *Jāmi' at-Tirmidhī*, vol. 1/p. 72 (#481); at-Tabarānī in *Musnad al-Shamiyyīn* (#885); and al-Bayhaqī in *Shu'ab al-Īmān,* vol. 7/p. 138 (#9762).

[36] The minimum number of cycles for *Salāh ad-Duhā* is two and the maximum is twelve.

[37] *Jami' al-Tirmidhī*, vol. 12/ p. 17 (#472); *Sunan Ibn Mājah*, vol. 1/p. 99.

This species from the unseen realm will actually "start to burn if they approach the said person."[38]

COMMENTARY ENDS

---

[38] See *Lawāqih al-Anwār al-Qudsiyyah fī Bayān al-'Uhūd al-Muhammadiyyah*, p. 81.

Supplications for the Morning

Morning extends from the middle of the night until sunrise.

(1) This *du'ā* protects the supplicant from Shaytān, the accursed:[39]

$$بِسْمِ اللهِ الرَّحْمٰنِ الرَّحِيْمِ وَ لَا حَوْلَ وَ لَا قُوَّةَ اِلاَّ بِاللهِ الْعَلِيِّ الْعَظِيْمِ$$

Bismillāhir Rahmānir Rahīm. Wa lā hawla wa lā quwwata illa billāhil 'Aliyyil 'Azīm.

In the Name of Allāh, the Most Gracious, the Most Merciful. And there is no might, nor power except from Allāh, the Most High, the Supreme.

(2) [Similarly,] if the supplicant recites Sūrah 112: al-Ikhlās eleven times [in the morning] it will protect him from Shaytān, the accursed.

---

[39] *Madārij al-Nubuwwah*, vol. 1/p. 425; Imām an-Nabhānī's *Afdal al-Salāh 'alā Sayyid al-Sādāt*, p. 166.

(3) Read this supplication to increase one's faith [*īmān*]. It should be recited forty-one times [in the morning]: [40]

$$يَا حَىُّ يَا قَيُّوْمُ لاَ اِلٰهَ اِلاَّ اَنْتَ$$

Yā Hayyu Yā Qayyumu lā ilāha illa anta.

O Ever-Living One! O Eternally Self-Sustaining One! There is no one worthy of worship except You.

(4) This *du'ā* will protect one from insanity, leprosy and blindness. It should be read three times: [41]

---

[40] This supplication is recorded in *Kanz al-'Ummāl* (#3266); and part of the narration reads: "Your Lord is the Ever-Living, the Most Generous. Indeed, Allāh is Shy and Beneficent. He is Shy when His servant raises his hands unto Him (in supplication) to return them empty, disappointed! Therefore, whenever you lift-up your hands in supplication recite the following *du'ā* three times Yā Hayyu Yā Qayyum lā ilāha illa anta. Once you have finished this prayer of supplication distribute your blessings by rubbing your hands over your face." It is also mentioned in *al-Risālāh* of Imām al-Qushayrī from Abū 'Alī al-Kutāmī ☙, who narrates: "I saw the Messenger of Allāh ☙ in my dream so I beseeched him with this plea: 'O Messenger of Allāh ☙, make *du'ā* to Allāh that my heart never becomes spiritually dead.' The Messenger of Allāh ☙ replied, 'If you desire that Allāh keep your heart alive [in His remembrance] and thus it never dies, then recite Yā Hayyu Yā Qayyum lā ilāha illa anta forty-one times every day.'" (There is a reference for this narration in *al-Risālāh al-Qushayrīyah* to page 520 of Imām an-Nabhānī's *Sa'ādah al-Dārayn*.)

[41] *Sahīh al-Bukhārī*, vol. 2/p. 948; *Sahīh Muslim*, vol. 2/p. 351; *Sunan Abū Dāwūd*; *Jāmi' al-Tirmidhī*, vol. 2/pp. 184-185; Ibn al-Sunnī's *'Amal al-*

$$\text{سُبْحَانَ اللهِ العَظِيْمِ وَ بِحَمْدِهِ}$$

SubhānAllāhil 'Azīm wa bi Hamdih.

Glory be to Allāh, the Supreme, and for Him is all praise.

(5) It should also be the priority of every disciple [*murīd*] to complete, at least, one Chapter [*Sūrah*] of the Holy Qur'ān every day before sunrise.

(6) The disciple [*murīd*] should also complete one part of the *Dalā'il al-Khayrāt* [The Guidebook of Blessings]. This famous book is a compendium of prayers and salutations

---

Yawm wa'l Laylah, p. 67; *Al-Hisn al-Hasīn*, p. 264. This report is also in *al-Mu'jam al-Kabīr* by at-Tabarānī from 'Abdullāh ibn 'Abbās ☈ who narrates: "Qabisah ibn Mukhariq al-Hilālī ☈ came to the Messenger of Allāh ☙ and greeted him with the greeting of peace. The Messenger of Allāh ☙ replied to his greeting and welcomed him and enquired: 'What has made you come here, O Qabisah?' He replied: 'O Messenger of Allāh, I've grown old, and my skin has become wrinkled. My body is weak and feeble, and I am now incapable of undergoing tasks which I could easily accomplish before.' Thus, the Messenger of Allāh ☙ [gave me a remedy by] teaching me some words of supplication so that Allāh Most High would grant me benefit through them.' He ☙ said: 'O Qabisah, when you have performed the morning prayer [*salāh*], then read the following supplication three times *SubhānAllāhi wa bi-Hamdihi SubhānAllāhil 'Azīmi wa bi-Hamdihi wa la hawla wa la quwwata illa Billah.* If you state these words, then you shall be safeguarded from losing your eyesight and catching leprosy by the Will of Allāh Most High...'"

56

upon the Prophet ﷺ [*durūd sharīf*] authored by Imām Muhammad ibn Sulaymān al-Jazūlī ؓ (d. 870/1465).[42] [The translator has provided a brief commentary on the *Dalā'il al-Khayrāt* in the appendix of this book.]

(7) After the Fajr prayer, the disciple [*murīd*] should recite the litany of the chain of transmission [*shajarah sharīf*].[43]

---

[42] *Fatāwā al-Radawiyyah*, vol. 10/p. 149.
[43] See Sayyidī al-Shaykh Abu'l Husayn Ahmad al-Nūrī Marahrāwī's ؓ *Sirāj al-'Awārif fil Wasāyā wal Ma'ārif*, p. 165.

Supplications for the Morning and the Afternoon

Morning extends from the middle of the night till sunrise, and afternoon is a period from midday till the sun sets.

(1) Reciting the following *du'ā* once in the morning and once in the evening will protect the supplicant from every disease and calamity especially from leprosy, blindness and paralysis:[44]

سُبْحٰنَ اللهِ وَ بِحَمْدِه مَا شَاءَ اللهُ كَانَ وَ مَا لَمْ يَشَأْ لَمْ يَكُنْ اَعْلَمُ أَنَّ اللهَ عَلَى كُلِّ شَىْءٍ قَدِيرٌ وَّ أَنَّ اللهَ قَدْ اَحَاطَ بِكُلِّ شَىْءٍ عِلْمًا

SubhanAllāhi wa bi-hamdihi wa lā Hawla wa la Quwwata illa billāhi māsha-Allāhu kāna wa mā lam yasha' lam yakun a'lamu annAllāha 'alā kulli shay'in Qadīr. Wa annAllāha qad Ahāta bi kulli shay'in 'ilmā.

---

[44] *Sunan Abū Dāwūd*, p. 353 (#5075); an-Nasā'ī (#12); *Mishkāt al-Masābīh*, p. 210; Ibn al-Sunnī in his *'Amal al-Yawm wa'l Laylah*, p. 72 (#46); Abū Nu'aym.

Glory be to Allāh and all praise. There is no might, nor power except from Allāh. Whatever He wished has happened, and whatever He has not wished has not happened. I know that indeed Allāh is Powerful over all things, and that indeed Allāh encompasses all things in His Knowledge.

(2) Reciting the following Qur'ānic verses will further safeguard the supplicant from all calamities. First read the Verse of the Throne [*Āyat al-Kursī*][45] once:

اللَّهُ لَا إِلَـٰهَ إِلَّا هُوَ ٱلْحَىُّ ٱلْقَيُّومُ ۚ لَا تَأْخُذُهُۥ سِنَةٌ وَلَا نَوْمٌ ۚ لَّهُۥ مَا فِى ٱلسَّمَـٰوَٰتِ وَمَا فِى ٱلْأَرْضِ ۗ مَن ذَا ٱلَّذِى يَشْفَعُ عِندَهُۥٓ إِلَّا بِإِذْنِهِۦ ۚ يَعْلَمُ مَا بَيْنَ أَيْدِيهِمْ وَمَا خَلْفَهُمْ ۖ وَلَا يُحِيطُونَ بِشَىْءٍ مِّنْ عِلْمِهِۦٓ إِلَّا بِمَا شَآءَ ۚ وَسِعَ كُرْسِيُّهُ ٱلسَّمَـٰوَٰتِ وَٱلْأَرْضَ ۖ وَلَا يَـُٔودُهُۥ حِفْظُهُمَا ۚ وَهُوَ ٱلْعَلِىُّ ٱلْعَظِيمُ ۝

Allāhu lā ilāha 'illā huwa'l-Hayyul-Qayyūm. Lā ta'-khuzuhū sina-tunw-wa lā nawm. Lahū mā fīs-Samāwāti wa mā fīl-'ard. Man-Dhālladhī yashfa-'u 'indahū illā bī-idhnih. Ya-'lamu mā bayna aydīhim wa mā khalfahum. Wa lā yu-hītūna bi-shay-'im min 'il-mihī 'illā bimā shā'. Wa-si-'a Kursiyyu-hus-

---

[45] Sūrah al-Baqarah, 2:255.

Samāwā-ti wāl-'ard; wa lā ya-'ūdu-hu hifzu-humā wa Huwal-'Aliyyul-'Azīm.

Allāh, there is no god but He, the Living, the Everlasting. Slumber seizes Him not, neither sleep; to Him belongs all that is in the heavens and the earth. Who is there that shall intercede with Him save by His leave? He knows what lies before them and what is after them, and they comprehend not anything of His knowledge save such as He wills. His Throne comprises the heavens and earth; the preserving of them oppresses Him not; He is the All-High, the All-Glorious.

Then read the first three verses from Sūrah 40: al-Ghāfir once. But remember to begin in the Name of Allāh, the Most Gracious, the Most Merciful:

بِسْمِ اللهِ الرَّحْمٰنِ الرَّحِيْمِ

حٰمٓ ۞ تَنزِيلُ ٱلْكِتَٰبِ مِنَ ٱللَّهِ ٱلْعَزِيزِ ٱلْعَلِيمِ ۞ غَافِرِ ٱلذَّنۢبِ وَقَابِلِ ٱلتَّوْبِ شَدِيدِ ٱلْعِقَابِ ذِى ٱلطَّوْلِ لَآ إِلَٰهَ إِلَّا هُوَ إِلَيْهِ ٱلْمَصِيرُ ۞

Bismillāhir Rahmānir Rahīm
Hā Mīm. Tanzīlul Kitāb minAllahil 'Azīzil 'Alīm
Ghāfiridh Dhanb wa Qābilit Tawb Shadīdil 'Iqāb
Dhit-Tawl Lā-Ilaha Illā Hū Ilayhil Masīr

Hā Mīm. The revelation of the Book is from Allāh, the Most Honorable, the All-Knowing, the Forgiver of sin, the Acceptor of repentance, the Stern in punishment, the Bountiful. There is no God except Him; towards Him is the journeying.

(3) By reciting the three Quls[46] three times a Muslim will be protected throughout the day and during the afternoon. These verses will suffice him for his needs, too:[47]

قُلْ هُوَ ٱللَّهُ أَحَدٌ ۞ ٱللَّهُ ٱلصَّمَدُ ۞ لَمْ يَلِدْ وَلَمْ يُولَدْ ۞
وَلَمْ يَكُن لَّهُۥ كُفُوًا أَحَدُۢ ۞

Qul Huw Allāhu 'Ahad. Allāhus-Samad. Lam yalid, wa lam yūlad. Walam yakul-la-hū kufuwan ahad.

Say: "He is Allāh, the One and Only; Allāh, the Eternal, Absolute; He begetteth not, nor is He begotten; and there is none like unto Him."

قُلْ أَعُوذُ بِرَبِّ ٱلْفَلَقِ ۞ مِن شَرِّ مَا خَلَقَ ۞ وَمِن شَرِّ غَاسِقٍ
إِذَا وَقَبَ ۞ وَمِن شَرِّ ٱلنَّفَّٰثَٰتِ فِي ٱلْعُقَدِ ۞ وَمِن شَرِّ
حَاسِدٍ إِذَا حَسَدَ ۞

---

46 Sūrah 112: al-Ikhlās, Sūrah 113: al-Falaq, and Sūrah 114: an-Nās.
47 *Jāmi' at-Tirmidhī*, p.198; *Sunan Abū Dāwūd*, p. 354.

Qul 'a-ūdhu bi-Rabbil-Falaq. Min-sharri mā khalaq.
Wa min-sharri gāsiqin idhā waqab. Wa min-
sharrin-Naffāthāti fīl–'uqad. Wa min-sharri ḫāsidin
'idhā ḫasad.

Say: "I seek refuge with the Lord of the Dawn.
From the mischief of created things; from the
mischief of darkness as it overspreads; and from the
mischief of the envious one as he practices envy."

قُلْ أَعُوذُ بِرَبِّ ٱلنَّاسِ ۝ مَلِكِ ٱلنَّاسِ ۝ إِلَٰهِ ٱلنَّاسِ ۝
مِن شَرِّ ٱلْوَسْوَاسِ ٱلْخَنَّاسِ ۝ ٱلَّذِى يُوَسْوِسُ فِى صُدُورِ
ٱلنَّاسِ ۝ مِنَ ٱلْجِنَّةِ وَٱلنَّاسِ ۝

Qul 'a-'ūdhu bi-Rabbin-Nās. Malikin-Nās, 'llāhin-
Nās. Min-sharril-Waswāsil-khan-Nās, alladhī
yuwas-wisu fī sudūrin-Nās, Minal-Jinnati wan-
Nās.

Say: "I seek refuge with the Lord and Cherisher of
men, the King of men, the God of men, from the
mischief of him, who breathes temptations into the
minds of men, who whispers evil thoughts to the
hearts of men, from among the Jinns and men."

(4) The following *du'ā* protects a Muslim from seven things: fire, drowning, theft, snakes, scorpions, Shaytān, and tyrannical rulers. It should be recited three times:[48]

بِسْمِ اللهِ مَا شَآءَ اللهُ لَا يَسُوْقُ الْخَيْرَ اِلاَّ اللهُ مَا شَآءَ اللهُ لاَ يَصْرِفُ السُّوَءَ اِلاَّ اللهُ مَا شَآءَ اللهُ مَا كَانَ مِنْ نِّعْمَةٍ فَمِنَ اللهِ مَا شَآءَ اللهُ لاَ حَوْلَ وَ لاَ قُوَّةَ اِلاَّ بِاللهِ

Bismillāhi mashā Allāhu lā yasūqul khayra ill Allāhu ma-shā Allāhu lā yasrifus Sū'a ill Allāhu ma-shā Allāhu ma kāna min ni'matin fa min-Allāhi ma-shā Allāhu lā Hawla wa lā Quwwata illa billāh.

In the Name of Allāh, we seek blessings and assistance from whatever Allāh wills. No one brings good except Allāh, however much Allāh wills. No one averts evil except Allāh, however

---

[48] This supplication has been cited by Hujjat al-Islām Abū Hāmid al-Ghazzālī in *Ihyā' 'Ulūm ad-Dīn* (Beirut: Dar al-Ma'rifah, n.d.), vol. 1/p. 328; Imām Jalāl ad-Dīn 'Abd ar-Rahmān as-Suyūtī in *Dalā'il al-Falāh fī Adhkār al-Masā' was-Sabāh*; and Ibn 'Adī in *al-Kāmil*, vol. 2/p. 740. Al-'Uqayli in *al-Du'afā'*, vol. 1; and others, who narrate with their chains of transmission from Muhammad ibn Ahmad ibn Zabda ﷺ, who states, "We were informed by 'Amr ibn 'Asim from al-Hasan ibn Razin who narrates from Ibn Jurayj who narrates from 'Ata ibn Rabah who narrates from Sayyidunā 'Abdullāh ibn 'Abbās who narrates from the Messenger of Allāh ﷺ who said, 'Each year Khidr ﷺ and Ilyas ﷺ meet in the season of Hajj. [Upon completing the rites of Pilgrimage] they shave one another's head and depart by saying these words [as specified in the aforementioned *du'ā*].'" Ibn Hibbān's version is narrated on the authority of Ibn Zayd ﷺ.

much Allāh wills. Whatever bounty there is, it is from Allāh, however much Allāh wills. There is no might, nor power except from Allāh.

(5) This *du'ā* also protects the supplicant from snakes, reptiles and other harmful things. It should be recited three times:[49]

أَعُوذُ بِكَلِمْاتِ اللهِ التَّامَّاتِ مِنْ شَرِّ مَا خَلَقَ

A'ūdhū bi kalimātil lāhit tāmmāti min sharri ma khalaq.

I seek refuge in the perfect words of Allāh from the evil of what He has created.

(6) This *du'ā* protects you against any poison and its sort. It should be recited three times:[50]

بِسْمِ اللهِ الَّذِيْ لاَ يَضُرُّ مَعَ اسْمِهِ شَيْئٌ فِى الأَرْضِ وَ لاَ فِى السَّمَآءِ وَ هُوَ السَّمِيْعُ الْعَلِيْمُ

---

[49] *Sahīh Muslim*, vol. 2/p. 347 (#2709); *Sunan Abū Dāwūd* (#3898); *Musnad Ahmad*, vol. 2/p. 290, vol. 3/p. 442, and vol. 5/p. 430; *Sunan Ibn Mājah* (#3518); an-Nasā'ī in his *'Amal al-Yawm wa'l Laylah* (#585-592); and Ibn al-Sunnī in his *'Amal al-Yawm wa'l Laylah* (#712).

[50] *Sunan Abū Dāwūd* (#5088-5089); *Jāmi' at-Tirmidhī* (#3385); *Sunan Ibn Mājah* (#3869); *Musnad Ahmad*, vol. 1/p. 62-63; an-Nasā'ī in *'Amal al-Yawm wa'l Laylah* (#15-16, 346-347) with an authentic chain of narration; *Sahīh Ibn Hibbān* (#2532); and *al-Mustadrak* by al-Hākim, vol. 1/p. 514.

Bismillā hil ladhī lā yadurru ma'asmihi shay-un fil ardi wa lā fis samā' wa Huwas Samī'ul 'Alīm.

In the Name of Allāh, by Whose Name nothing harms on earth, or in the heavens; and He is the All-Hearing, the All-Knowing.

(7) This *du'ā* assures a person that Allāh Almighty will be pleased with him on the Day of Judgment. It should be read three times:[51]

رَضِيتُ بِاللهِ رَبَّا وَّ بِالإسْلاَمِ دِينَا وَّ بِسَيِّدِنَا وَّ مَوْلاَنَا مُحَمَّدٍ صَلَّى اللهُ تَعَالَى عَلَيْهِ وَ سَلَّمَ نَبِيًّا وَّ رَسُوْلاً

Radītu billāhi Rabbaw wa bil-Islami Dīnaw wa bi Sayyidina wa Mawlānā Muhammadin sall-Allāhu 'alayhi wa sallam Nabiyyaw wa Rasūla.

I am content with Allāh as my Lord, Islam as my religion, and with Muhammad ﷺ as His Prophet and Messenger.

(8) This *du'ā* protects the supplicant from all ills and torments. Recite it ten times [in the morning and the

---

[51] *Sahīh Muslim* (#1884); *Sunan al-Tirmidhī*, vol. 2 (#3386); *Sunan Abū Dāwūd*, vol. 2/p. 352 (#1529, 5072); *Sunan an-Nasā'ī al-Sughrā*, vol. 6/p. 19-20; an-Nasā'ī also related this tradition in his *'Amal al-Yawm wa'l Laylah* (#4, 565); Ibn al-Sunnī in *'Amal al-Yawm wa'l Laylah* (#68); *Musnad Ahmad*, vol. 3/p. 214, vol. 4/p. 337, and vol. 5/p. 367; and *al-Mustadrak* by al-Hākim, vol. 1/p. 518.

afternoon]:[52]

$$ حَسْبِيَ اللهُ لاَ اِلهَ اِلاَّ هُوَ عَلَيْهِ تَوَكَّلْتُ وَ هُوَ رَبُّ الْعَرْشِ الْعَظِيْمِ $$

Hasbiy-Allāhu lā ilāha illa Huwa 'alayhi tawakkaltu wa Huwa Rabbul 'Arshil 'Azīm.

Allāh is sufficient for me. There is none worthy of worship save Him. I have placed my trust in Him, and He is the Lord of the Majestic Throne.

(9) This *du'ā* [is a verse from the Holy Qur'ān (30:17-19) and] protects the supplicant from all ills during the day and night. It should be read once:[53]

$$ فَسُبْحَانَ اللّهِ حِينَ تُمْسُونَ وَحِينَ تُصْبِحُونَ ۞ وَلَهُ الْحَمْدُ فِى السَّمَوَاتِ وَالْأَرْضِ وَعَشِيًّا وَحِينَ تُظْهِرُونَ ۞ يُخْرِجُ الْحَىَّ مِنَ الْمَيِّتِ وَيُخْرِجُ الْمَيِّتَ مِنَ الْحَىِّ وَيُحْىِ الْأَرْضَ بَعْدَ مَوْتِهَا وَكَذَٰلِكَ تُخْرَجُونَ ۞ $$

---

[52] Ibn al-Sunnī in *'Amalul Yawm wal Laylah* (#70-71); *Sunan Abū Dāwūd* (#5081).

[53] *Sunan Abū Dāwūd*, vol. 2/p. 303 (#5076, 5090); *Musnad Ahmad*, vol. 2/p. 45; Khatīb at-Tabrīzī in his *Mishkāt al-Masābīh*, p. 210; an-Nasā'ī in *'Amal al-Yawm wa'l Laylah* (#22, 572); Ibn al-Sunnī in *'Amal al-Yawm wa'l Laylah* (#69).

Fa-SubhānAllāhi hīna tumsūna wa hīna tusbihūn. Wa lahul-Hamdu fissa-mā-wāti wal ardi wa 'ashīyyanw-wa hīna tuzhirūn. Yukhrijul-hayya minal-mayyit wa yukhrijul-mayyita minal-hayy wa yuh'yil-arda ba-'da mawtihā wa kadhā-lika tukhrajūn.

So glory be to Allāh, both in your evening hour and in your morning hour. His is the praise in the heavens and earth, alike at the setting sun and in your noontide hour. He brings forth the living from the dead, and brings forth the dead from the living, and He revives the earth after it is dead; even so you shall be brought forth.

(10) The recital of the last four verses of Sūrah 23: al-Mu'minūn protects one from Shaytān, the accursed, and evil Jinn—a species of the unseen realm, concealed from humans, though humans are not concealed from them. It should be read once:[54]

أَفَحَسِبْتُمْ أَنَّمَا خَلَقْنَٰكُمْ عَبَثًا وَأَنَّكُمْ إِلَيْنَا لَا تُرْجَعُونَ ۝

فَتَعَٰلَى ٱللَّهُ ٱلْمَلِكُ ٱلْحَقُّ لَآ إِلَٰهَ إِلَّا هُوَ رَبُّ ٱلْعَرْشِ ٱلْكَرِيمِ

۝ وَمَن يَدْعُ مَعَ ٱللَّهِ إِلَٰهًا ءَاخَرَ لَا بُرْهَٰنَ لَهُۥ بِهِۦ فَإِنَّمَا

---

54 Sūrah al-Mu'minūn, 23: 115-118. Ibn al-Sunnī in *'Amal al-Yawm wa'l Laylah* (#631).

حِسَابُهُۥ عِندَ رَبِّهِۦٓ إِنَّهُۥ لَا يُفْلِحُ ٱلْكَـٰفِرُونَ ۝ وَقُل رَّبِّ ٱغْفِرْ

وَٱرْحَمْ وَأَنتَ خَيْرُ ٱلرَّٰحِمِينَ ۝

Afahasibtum 'annamā khalaq-nākum 'abathaw wa 'annakum 'ilaynā lā turja-'ūn Fata-'ālAllāhul-Malikul-Haqq: Lā 'ilāha 'illā Hū: Rabbul-'Arshil-Karīm. Wa may-yad'u ma'-Allāhi 'ilāhan Ākhara lā burhāna lahū bihī fa-'innamā hisābuhū 'inda Rabbih 'Innahū lā yuflihul-Kāfirūn! Wa Qur-Rabbigh-fir warham wa 'Anta Khayrur-Rāhimīn!

What, did you think that We created you only for sport, and that you would not be returned to Us? Then high exalted be Allāh, the King, the True! There is no god but He, the Lord of the Majestic Throne. And whosoever calls upon another god with Allāh, whereof he has no proof, his reckoning is with his Lord; surely the non-believers shall not prosper. And say (O beloved Messenger ﷺ): "My Lord, forgive and have mercy,[55] for Thou art the best of the merciful."

(11) The recital of "*A'ūdhu bil-lāhis Samī'il 'Alīmi minash-Shaytānir-rajīm* [I seek refuge in Allāh, the All-Hearing, the

---

[55] Allāh's Messenger ﷺ offered this supplication either on behalf of his own Community or for all the believers, including those from the previous Communities. This Qur'ānic *du'ā* may be used as evidence for the Prophet's ﷺ intercession (*Tafsīr Nūr-ul-Irfān*, vol. 2/p. 56).

All-Knowing, from Shaytān, the accursed]" three times
followed by the last three verses of Sūrah 59: al-Hashr
assures the supplicant that 70,000 angels pray for his
forgiveness:[56]

اَعُوْذُ بِاللهِ السَّمِيْعِ الْعَلِيْمِ مِنَ الشَّيْطَانِ الرَّجِيْمِ

هُوَ ٱللَّهُ ٱلَّذِى لَآ إِلَٰهَ إِلَّا هُوَ ۖ عَٰلِمُ ٱلْغَيْبِ وَٱلشَّهَٰدَةِ ۖ هُوَ
ٱلرَّحْمَٰنُ ٱلرَّحِيمُ ﴿٢٢﴾ هُوَ ٱللَّهُ ٱلَّذِى لَآ إِلَٰهَ إِلَّا هُوَ ٱلْمَلِكُ
ٱلْقُدُّوسُ ٱلسَّلَٰمُ ٱلْمُؤْمِنُ ٱلْمُهَيْمِنُ ٱلْعَزِيزُ ٱلْجَبَّارُ
ٱلْمُتَكَبِّرُ ۚ سُبْحَٰنَ ٱللَّهِ عَمَّا يُشْرِكُونَ ﴿٢٣﴾ هُوَ ٱللَّهُ
ٱلْخَٰلِقُ ٱلْبَارِئُ ٱلْمُصَوِّرُ ۖ لَهُ ٱلْأَسْمَآءُ ٱلْحُسْنَىٰ ۚ يُسَبِّحُ لَهُۥ مَا فِى
ٱلسَّمَٰوَٰتِ وَٱلْأَرْضِ ۖ وَهُوَ ٱلْعَزِيزُ ٱلْحَكِيمُ ﴿٢٤﴾

A'ūdhu bil-lāhis Samī'il 'Alīmi minash-Shaytānir-
rajīm.

HuwAllāhul-ladhi Lā-'ilāha 'illā Hū; 'Ālimul-
ghaybi wash-shahādah; Huwar-Rahmānur-
Rahīm.HuwAllāhul-ladhi Lā-'i-lāha 'illā Hū; al-
Malikul Quddūsus-Salāmul-Mu'minul-Muhay-

---

[56] Sūrah al-Hashr, 59:22-24. *Jāmi' al-Tirmidhī*, vol. 2/p. 120 (#2963); ad-
Dārimī in his *Sunan* (#3426); Ibn al-Sunnī in *'Amal al-Yawm wa'l Laylah*
(#681); *al-Hisn al-Hasīn*, p. 61-62.

minul-ʿAzīzul-Jabbārul-Mutakabbir: SubhānAllāhi
ʿammā yushrikūn. HuwAllāhul-Khāliqul-Bāri-ʾul-
Musawwiru lahul-ʿAsmā-ʾul-Husnā: yusabbihu
lahū mā fis-samāwāti wal-ʿard wa Huwal-ʿAzīzul-
Hakīm.

I seek refuge in Allāh, the All-Hearing, the All-
Knowing, from Shaytān, the accursed.

He is Allāh, besides Whom there is none to be
worshipped, the Knower of everything hidden and
open. He is the Most Affectionate, the Most
Merciful. He is Allāh, besides Whom none is to be
worshipped—the Sovereign, the Holy One, the
Bestower of Peace, the Guardian of Faith, the Giver
of Security, the Protector, the Esteemed One, the
Exalted, the Majestic. Glory is to Allāh! (High is He)
above the partners they attribute to Him. He is
Allāh, the Maker, the Creator, the Fashioner. To
Him belong the Most Beautiful Names: all that is in
the heavens and the earth glorifies Him: and He is
the Esteemed One, the Wise.

(12) One who reads this *duʿā* is assured that he will depart
this mundane world with faith [*īmān*]. It should be read
three times:[57]

---

[57] *Jāmiʿ at-Tirmidhī*, vol. 3/p. 120.

اَللّٰهُمَّ اِنَّا نَعُوْذُ بِكَ مِنْ اَنْ نُّشْرِكَ بِكَ شَيْئًا نَّعْلَمُهٗ
وَ نَسْتَغْفِرُكَ لِمَا لاَ نَعْلَمُهٗ

Allāhumma innā na'ūdhu bika min an nushrika
bika shay'an na'lamuhu wa nastaghfiruka lima lā
na'lamah.

O Allāh I seek refuge in You from associating
partners with You in anything knowingly, and I
seek Your forgiveness for that which I commit
unknowingly.

(13) This *du'ā* protects one's faith [*īmān*], religion [*dīn*], life
and wealth. It should be read three times:[58]

بِسْمِ اللهِ عَلٰى دِيْنِىْ بِسْمِ اللهِ عَلٰى نَفْسِىْ وَ وُلْدِىْ وَ
اَهْلِىْ وَ مَالِىْ

---

[58] Narrated in *Kanz al-'Ummāl* (#4958) from 'Abdullāh ibn Mas'ūd ﷺ,
who said: "A man came to the noble Prophet ﷺ and said: 'O Messenger
of Allāh ﷺ, by Allāh, I fear for my children, my family and my wealth.'
The Messenger of Allāh ﷺ replied: 'Say: *Bismillāhi 'alā dīnī wa nafsī wa
wuldī wa ahlī wa mālī* in the morning and the evening.' So the man
recited these words regularly in the morning and the evening. After a
while, he came back to the Holy Prophet ﷺ who asked him: 'What
happened to the fear that you once felt?' The man answered: 'By the
One Who has sent you with the Truth, whatever fear I had, it has
completely been removed from me.'" Ibn al-Sunnī also narrated this
du'ā in *'Amal al-Yawm wa'l Laylah*, p. 74; as did Imām Yūsuf ibn Ismā'īl
an-Nabhānī in his *al-Fath al-Kabīr fī damm al-Ziyādati ilā al-Jāmi' al-
Saghīr*, vol. 2/p. 284.

Bismillāhi 'alā dīnī bismillāhi 'alā nafsī wa wuldī wa ahlī wa mālī.

In the Name of Allāh, I seek blessings and assistance in my religion. In the Name of Allāh, I seek blessings and assistance with myself, my children, my family, and my wealth.

(14) This *du'ā* is to show gratitude to Allāh, Almighty & Glorious is He, for all that the supplicant has received. If he recites it in the afternoon, then 'evening' [*amsā*] must be said in place of 'morning' [*asbaha*]. It should be read once:[59]

اَللّٰهُمَّ مَا أَصْبَحَ [أَمْسٰى] بِىْ مِنْ نِّعْمَةٍ اَوْ بِاَحَدٍ مِّنْ خَلْقِكَ فَمِنْكَ وَحْدَكَ لاَ شَرِيْكَ لَكَ فَلَكَ الْحَمْدُ وَ لَكَ الشُّكْرُ ۔ لاَ اِلٰهَ اِلاَّ اَنْتَ سُبْحَانَكَ اِنِّى كُنْتُ مِنَ الظَّالِمِيْنَ

Allāhumma mā asbaha [amsā] bī min ni'matin aw bi ahadim min khalqik fa minka Wahdaka lā sharīka lak falakal Hamdu wa-lakash Shukr. Lā ilāha illa Anta Subhānaka innī kuntu minaz-zālimīn.

---

[59] *Sunan Abū Dāwūd*, p. 352 (#5073); *Sahīh Ibn Hibbān* (#2361); *Mishkāt al-Masābīh*, p. 211; an-Nasā'ī in his *'Amal al-Yawm wa'l Laylah* (#7); Ibn al-Sunnī in his *'Amal al-Yawm wa'l Laylah* (#41); *Sunan al-Tirmidhī*, p. 188.

O Allāh, whatever blessings have come to me or to someone from Your creation in the morning [or: evening], then it is from You, the One Who has no partner, for You is all praise and gratitude. There is no one worthy of worship except You, surely I am from the wrongdoers.

(15) This *du'ā* protects the supplicant against Shayṭān, the accursed, and his minions. It should be read once:[60]

بِسْمِ اللهِ ذِى الْشَّأْنِ عَظِيْمِ الْبُرْهَانِ شَدِيْدِ السُّلْطَانِ مَا شَآءَ اللهُ كَانَ اَعُوْذُ بِاللهِ مِنَ الشَّيْطَانِ الرَّجِيْمِ

Bismillāhi Dhish Sha'ni 'Azīmil Burhān Shadīdis Sultān Mashā-Allāhu kān A'ūdhu Billāhi minash Shayṭānir-rajīm.

In the Name of Allāh, the Sultān of supreme honor, splendor, and authority. Everything is in accordance with the determination and will of Allāh, and His will is fulfilled. I seek refuge in Allāh from Shayṭān, the cursed.

(16) This *du'ā* should be read four times and with every recital, one quarter of the body becomes safe from the fire of Hell. If the supplicant reads this *du'ā* in the afternoon,

---

[60] Narrated in *Kanz al-'Ummāl* (#3862) and in *Musnad al-Firdaws* from Zubayr ibn al-'Awwam ﷺ (#6054). It is also cited in *Ghunyatut Tālibīn*, p. 575 (Urdu).

then in place of 'morning' [*asbahtu*] he should read 'evening' [*amsaytu*]:[61]

اَللّٰهُمَّ اِنِّى اَصْبَحْتُ [أَمْسَيْتُ] اُشْهِدُكَ وَ اُشْهِدُ حَمَلَةَ عَرْشِكَ وَ مَلَائِكَتَكَ وَ جَمِيعَ خَلْقِكَ اَنَّكَ اَنْتَ اللّٰهُ لاَ اِلٰهَ اِلاَّ اَنْتَ وَحْدَكَ لاَ شَرِيْكَ لَكَ وَ اَنَّ مُحَمَّدًا عَبْدُكَ وَ رَسُوْلُكَ

Allāhumma innī asbahtu [amsaytu] ush'hiduka wa ush'hidu Hamalata 'Arshik wa Malā'ikatak wa jamī'a khalqik annaka antAllāhu lā ilāha illa Anta Wahdaka lā sharīka lak wa anna Muhamaddan 'Abduk wa Rasūluk Sall-Allāhu 'alayhi wa Sallam.

O Allāh, I enter the morning [or: evening] bearing witness before You – and before the carriers of Your Throne, all of Your angels, and all of creation – that You are God; there is no god but You alone, without partner, and that Muhammad is Your servant and messenger.

(17) This *du'ā* is equal to an entire day's worship ['*ibādah*]. It should be read once:[62]

---

[61] *Sunan Abū Dāwūd* (#5069); *Jāmi' al-Tirmidhī*, vol. 2/p. 187 (#3495); al-Bukhārī in *al-Ādāb al-Mufrad* (#1201); an-Nasā'ī in *'Amal al-Yawm wa'l Laylah* (#9-10); Ibn al-Sunnī in *'Amal al-Yawm wa'l Laylah* (#69); *Mishkāt al-Masābīh*, p. 210.

اَللّٰهُمَّ لَكَ الْحَمْدُ حَمْدًا دَائِمًا مَّعَ دَوَامِكَ وَ لَكَ
الْحَمْدُ حَمْدًا خَالِدًا مَعَ خُلُوْدِكَ وَ لَكَ الْحَمْدُ حَمْدًا
لاَّ مُنْتَهَى لَهُ دُوْنَ مَشِيَّتِكَ وَ لَكَ الْحَمْدُ حَمْدًا لاَّ
يُرِيْدُ قَائِلُهُ اِلاَّ رِضَاكَ وَ لَكَ الْحَمْدُ حَمْدًا عِنْدَ كُلِّ
طَرَفَةِ عَيْنٍ وَّ تَنَفُّسِ كُلِّ نَفَسٍ

Allāhumma lakal hamdu hamdan dā'imam ma'a
dawāmik wa lakal hamdu hamdan khālidan ma'a
Khulūdik wa lakal hamdu hamdal lā muntahā lahu
dūna mashiyyatika wa lakal hamdu hamdan 'inda
kulli tarafati 'ayniw wa tanaffusi kulli nafas.

O Allāh for You is all praise, such a praise that is
everlasting with Your permanence. And for You is
all praise, such that is infinite with Your
immortality. And for You is all praise, such that has
no limit. And for You is all praise, such that its
writer does not intend through it save Your
pleasure. And for You is all praise upon every
blinking of an eye and at the time of respiration of
every breath.

---

[62] There are Hadīth narrations that convey the general meaning of this
du'ā like *Kanz al-'Ummal*, vol. 2/pp. 99, 104, and 269; *Majma' al-Zawaid
wa Manba' al-Fawaid*, vol. 10/p. 97.

(18) This *du'ā* should be read eleven times for help in repaying debts and once for the removal of any anguish:[63]

اَللّٰهُمَّ اِنِّى اَعُوْذُ بِكَ مِنَ الْهَمِّ وَ الْحُزْنِ وَ اَعُوْذُ بِكَ مِنَ الْعَجْزِ وَ الْكَسَلِ وَ اَعُوْذُ بِكَ مِنَ الْجُبْنِ وَ الْبُخْلِ وَ اَعُوْذُ بِكَ مِنْ غَلَبَةِ الدَّيْنِ وَ قَهْرِ الرِّجَالِ

Allāhumma innī a'ūdhu-bika minal hammi wal huzn wa a'ūdhu-bika minal 'ajzi wal kasal wa a'ūdhu-bika minal jubni wal bukhl wa a'ūdhu-bika min ghalabatid-dayn wa qahrir rijāl.

O Allāh, I seek refuge in You from all anxiety and grief, and I seek refuge in You from all weakness and indolence, and I seek refuge in You from cowardice and covetousness, and I seek refuge in You from overwhelming debt and from the overpowering of men.

(19) If a supplicant desires his work to be performed in a satisfactory manner, then he should read this *du'ā* once:[64]

---

[63] *Sunan Abū Dāwūd* (#1555); *Mishkāt al-Masābīh*, p. 215; *al-Hisn al-Hasīn*, p. 74.

[64] An-Nasā'ī in *'Amal al-Yawm wa'l Laylah* (#570); *al-Hisn al-Hasīn*, p. 70; Ibn al-Sunnī in *'Amal al-Yawm wa'l Laylah*, p. 73 (#48); *Jāmi' al-Tirmidhī*, vol. 2/p. 192; *Mishkāt al-Masābīh*, p. 216; *Sunan Abū Dāwūd*, p. 355; al-Hākim in his *al-Mustadrak*, vol. 1/p. 545.

يَا حَىُّ يَا قَيُّوْمُ بِرَحْمَتِكَ اَسْتَغِيْثُ فَلاَ تَكِلْنِى اِلٰى نَفْسِى طَرَفَةَ عَيْنٍ وَّ اَصْلِحْ لِىْ شَأْنِى كُلَّهُ

Yā Hayyu Yā Qayyūm bi Rahmatika astaghīth falā takilnī ilā nafsī tarafata 'ayn wa aslih li shā'ni kullah.

O Ever-Living Sustainer, I seek succor through Your mercy, and I seek safety from Your punishment. Rectify all of my affairs and do not leave me to my own self or to anyone from Your creation even for the twinkling of an eye.

(20) This *du'ā* is a prayer for guidance [*istikhāra*] to Divine favor. It must be read seven times if the supplicant wants to receive a sign on a certain matter that he intends to perform:[65]

اَللّٰهُمَّ خِرْ لِى وَاخْتَرْ لِىْ وَ لاَ تَكِلْنِى اِلٰى اخْتِيَارِىْ

Allāhumma khir lī wakhtar-lī wa lā takilnī ila'khtiyārī.

O Allāh, choose for me that which is best, and do not entrust me to my own choice.

---

[65] *Jāmi' al-Tirmidhī*, p. 191 (#3432); *Musnad al-Bazzār*; Ibn al-Sunnī in his *'Amal al-Yawm wa'l Laylah*, p. 112.

(21) This *du'ā* is known as the Chief Prayer for Seeking Forgiveness [*Sayyid al-Istighfār*]. It can be read either once or thrice. It is so powerful that if a disciple [*murīd*] recites it, and then passes away on that day or night, he will be blessed with the status of a martyr [*shahīd*]:[66]

اَللّٰهُمَّ اَنْتَ رَبِّى لَا اِلٰهَ اِلاَّ اَنْتَ خَلَقْتَنِى وَ اَنَا عَبْدُكَ وَ اَنَا عَلٰى عَهْدِكَ وَ وَعْدِكَ مَا اسْتَطَعْتُ اَعُوْذُ بِكَ مِنْ شَرِّمَا صَنَعْتُ اَبُوْءُ لَكَ بِنِعْمَتِكَ عَلَىَّ وَ اَبُوْءُ لَكَ بِذَنْبِىْ فَاغْفِرْ لِىْ فَاِنَّهُ لاَ يَغْفِرُ الذُّنُوْبَ اِلاَّ اَنْتَ (وَاغْفِرْ لِكُلِّ مُؤْمِنٍ وَّ مُؤْمِنَةٍ)

Allāhumma anta Rabbī lā ilāha illa Anta khalaqtanī wa ana 'abduk wa ana 'alā 'Ahdik wa Wa'dik mastata't. A'ūdhū-bika min sharri ma sana't. Abū'u laka bi ni'matika 'alayy wa abū'u laka bi'dhanbī faghfirlī fa innahu lā yaghfirudh-Dhunūba illā Anta. (Waghfir li kulli mu'miniw wa mu'minah.)

O Allāh, You are my Lord; there is no God but You. You created me and I am Your slave. And Your covenant and promise I uphold to the best of my ability. And I seek refuge in You from the evil of whatever I have done. I acknowledge that all my

---

[66] *Sahīh al-Bukhārī*, vol. 2/p. 193 (#6306); *Jāmi' al-Tirmidhī*, p.176; *Sunan an-Nasā'ī al-Sughrā*, vol. 8/p. 279; *Musnad Ahmad*, vol. 4/pp. 122, 125; Ibn al-Sunnī in his *'Amal al-Yawm wa'l Laylah*, p. 67.

blessings are from You. And to You I bring my sins, so forgive me because no one can forgive sins but You. (And forgive all believing men and women.)

(22) This *du'ā* is a shield against hunger, fear in the grave, and the anxiety during the Day of Judgment [*qiyāmah*]. It should be read 100 times:[67]

$$ لَا اِلٰهَ اِلَّا اللّٰهُ الْمَلِكُ الْحَقُّ الْمُبِيْنُ $$

Lā ilāha ill Allāhul Malikul Haqqul Mubīn.

---

[67] Narrated in *Hilyat al-Awliyā'* by Imām Abū Nu'aym (vol. 8/p. 280) from Salim who narrated from Imām Mālik from Imām Ja'far ibn Muhammad from his father [Imām Muhammad Baqir] from his grandfather [Imām Husayn] who said: "I heard the Messenger of Allāh state: 'Anyone who recites *Lā ilāha ill Allāhul Malikul Haqqul Mubīn* 100 times every day, it shall grant him peace and comfort from the agonies of the grave, he shall be granted sustenance and affluence, and [through these words] he shall knock on the door of Paradise [*jannah*].'" It is also narrated in *Kanz al-'Ummāl* (#3896). According to the latter Hadīth: "'Abd Khayr said that 'Alī ibn Abī Tālib possessed four rings of sapphire for him to achieve his objective... upon it was engraved the words *Lā ilāha ill Allāhul Malikul Haqqul Mubīn*..." Imām as-Suyūtī has also narrated this Hadīth in his *Husul ar-Rifq bi-Usulir Rizq*. Likewise, Abū Nu'aym and al-Khatīb narrated this tradition related by Sayyidunā 'Alī from Mālik and ad-Daylamī in *Musnad al-Firdaws*. It is also cited in *Sa'ādatud Dārayn fis Salāhi 'alā Sayyidil Kawnayn*, p. 593; and *Madārij al-Nubuwwah*, vol. 1/p. 426.

There is no one worthy of worship except Allāh, the Sovereign, the Truth, the One Who makes things clear.

Supplications after the Fajr and Maghrib Prayers

(1) After performing the Fajr and Maghrib prayers, the supplicant should stay where he is seated and recite the following *du'ā* ten times. This prayer of supplication will protect him from Shaytān, the accursed, and assures that his sins are forgiven:[68]

لَا اِلٰهَ اِلَّا اللهُ وَحْدَهُ لَا شَرِيْكَ لَهُ لَهُ الْمُلْكُ وَلَهُ الْحَمْدُ بِيَدِهِ الْخَيْرُ يُحْيِ وَ يُمِيْتُ وَ هُوَ عَلَى كُلِّ شَىْءٍ قَدِيْرٌ

Lā ilāha illAllāhu Wahdahu lā sharīka lah lahul Mulku wa lahul Hamd bi-yadihil khayr Yuhyi wa Yumīt wa Huwa alā kulli shay'in Qadīr.

There is no one worthy of worship except Allāh, Who has no partner. For Him is all dominion and for Him is all praise. In His power is all good. He

---

[68] *Jāmi' al-Tirmidhī* (#3470, 3528); an-Nasā'ī in *'Amal al-Yawm wa'l Laylah* (#127, 577-578); *Sahīh Ibn Hibbān* (#2341).

grants life and gives death and He has power over everything.

(2) This *du'ā* should also be read seven times to protect the supplicant from the fire of Hell:[69]

اَللّٰهُمَّ اَجِرْنِیْ مِنَ النَّارِ

Allāhumma ajirnī minan Nār.

O Allāh, safeguard me from the fire of Hell.

(3) The supplicant should read the following litany [*wazīfah*] 350 times after the Maghrib prayer to protect his life, and wealth, and to attain divine blessings [*barakāt*], and spiritual insights:

حَسْبُنَا اللهُ وَ نِعْمَ الْوَكِيْلُ

---

[69] This *du'ā* is narrated from Walid ibn Muslim, who narrates from 'Abdur Rahman ibn Hassan al-Kinanī, who states that Muslim ibn Harith at-Tamimī narrated to him from his father, who said: "The Messenger of Allāh ﷺ told me: 'After you have performed the Fajr prayer recite *Allāhumma ajirni minan nār* seven times before you converse with anyone. If you die that day, then Allāh will protect you from the fire of Hell. And after you perform the Maghrib prayer recite *Allāhumma ajirni minan nār* seven times before you converse with anyone, because if you die that night, Allāh will protect you from the fire of Hell'" (*Musnad Ahmad*). It is also narrated by al-Bukhārī in *al-Tārīkh al-Kabīr*, vol. 7/p. 253; *Sunan Abū Dāwūd* (#5080); *Sahīh Ibn Hibbān* (#2022).

Hasbun Allāhu wa niʿmal Wakīl

Allāh is sufficient for us and He is the best disposer
of affairs.

The Prayer of Heedlessness

Once the supplicant has completed the recitation of litanies [*wazā'if*], then he should offer six cycles of supererogatory ritual prayer [*nafl salāh*] known as the prayer of heedlessness [*Salāh al-Awwabīn*], because of our tendency to be negligent of it due to lethargy or the like. *Salāh al-Awwabīn* is also called the prayer of those who oft-repent.

Translator's Commentary: It is interesting to note that whenever the paternal uncle of 'Abd ar-Rahmān ibn al-Aswad ﷺ would visit 'Abdullāh ibn Ma'sūd ﷺ, he would find him performing this voluntary ritual prayer. Ibn Ma'sūd ﷺ used to say: "It is (all too often) an hour of heedless neglect."[70] Abū Hurayrah ﷺ reports that the Messenger of Allāh ﷺ said: "Anyone who performs six cycles [*raka'āt*] after the Maghrib prayer and refrains from unworthy speech, they will be counted as equal in merit to the worshipful service [*'ibādah*] of twelve whole years."[71] Sayyidunā ash-Shaykh Muhyid'dīn 'Abd al-Qādir al-Jīlānī

---

[70] Shaykh 'Abd al-Qādir al-Jīlānī, *Sufficient Provisions for Seekers of the Path of Truth* (Hollywood: Al-Baz Publishing Inc., 1997), tr. Muhtar Holland, vol. 4/p. 30.

[71] Sadr al-'Ulamā Shaykh al-Sayyid Ghulām Jīlānī al-Merthī, *Islamic Laws & Etiquettes* [Nizām-e Sharī'at] (Bolton: Maktab-e-Qadriah, 2009), p. 373.

🕊 also reports the aforementioned Hadīth Sharīf in his *Sufficient Provisions for Seekers of the Path of Truth* as well as other Ahādīth including one on the authority of 'Abdullāh ibn 'Abbās 🕊, that the Prophet 🕊 once said: "If someone performs six cycles of [voluntary] ritual prayer [*sallā sitta raka'āt*], after the [prescribed prayer of] sunset [*ba'da'l-maghrib*] and before he has talked to anybody, they will be raised up for him to the Highest Heaven [*'Illiyūn*]. He will be just like someone who is present on the Night of Power [*Lailat al-Qadr*] in the Farthest Mosque [*al-Masjid al-Aqsā*], and that is better than devoting half a night to vigil."[72]

May Allāh the Exalted make us among those who turn to Him with supererogatory acts of worshipful service like Sayyidunā A'lāhadrat Imām Ahmad Ridā Khān al-Qādirī 🕊, āmīn.

COMMENTARY ENDS

---

[72] Shaykh 'Abd al-Qādir Jīlānī, *Sufficient Provisions for Seekers of the Path of Truth* (Hollywood: Al-Baz Publishing Inc., 1997), tr. Muhtar Holland, vol. 4/p. 28.

Supplications after the 'Ishā Prayer

(1) After offering the 'Ishā prayer, the supplicant should stand and turn toward the direction of Madinah the Illumined; thereafter, he should send the following blessings and salutations upon the Prophet ﷺ [durūd sharīf] with utmost respect. Do not read this durūd sharīf with the intention of traveling to visit [ziyārat] our Master, the Messenger of Allāh ﷺ, in the illumined city of Madinah. Rather the supplicant should believe that he will behold our liege-lord Muhammad ﷺ in his dreams [i.e., he will not have to wait for an undetermined period to make a journey, because he will have the honor of beholding the Prophet ﷺ immediately in his sleep. One should always aspire to visit the Chosen One ﷺ in the radiantly shinning city of Madinah. In this passage, the author is merely stressing the importance of establishing a link with the Prophet ﷺ in the present moment. It is a tremendous honor to behold Sayyidunā Muhammad ﷺ in a dream and a sign of spiritual proximity].

The supplicant should behave as though he is in front of the blessed sanctuary [ḥarām], and should stand with absolute reverence [and humility]. Read this durūd sharīf as much as possible, but be sure to end on an odd number of recitations such as three, nine, eleven, or thirty-three.[73]

$$\text{اَللّٰهُمَّ صَلِّ عَلٰى سَيِّدِنَا مُحَمَّدٍ كَمَا اَمَرْتَنَا اَنْ نُصَلِّىَ عَلَيْهِ}$$

Allāhumma Salli 'alā Sayyidinā Muhammadin kamā amartanā an nusalliya 'alayh.

O Allāh, bless our Master Muhammad as You have commanded us to send blessings upon him.

$$\text{اَللّٰهُمَّ صَلِّ عَلٰى سَيِّدِنَا مُحَمَّدٍ كَمَا هُوَ اَهْلُهُ}$$

Allāhumma Salli 'alā Sayyidinā Muhammadin kamā huwa ahluh.

O Allāh, bless our Master Muhammad as befitting with his noble state.

---

[73] Shaykh Abu'l Qasīm al-Subkī ﷺ in his *al-Durr al-Munazzam fi'l-Mawlid al-'Mu'azzam* relates through his chain that Allāh's Messenger ﷺ said: "Whosoever sends peace upon the blessed soul of Muhammad ﷺ from amongst the souls, and the blessed body of Muhammad ﷺ from the bodies, and on the blessed mausoleum of Muhammad ﷺ from amongst the graves, shall see me in his dream. And whosoever sees me in his dream shall see me on the Day of Reckoning, and whosoever sees me on the Day of Reckoning, I shall intercede for him, and for whosoever I intercede he shall drink from my Pond [al-kawthar] and Allāh shall forbid the fire of Hell from consuming him" (*Sa'ādah al-Dārayn*, p. 443).

اَللّٰهُمَّ صَلِّ عَلٰى سَيِّدِنَا مُحَمَّدٍ كَمَا تُحِبُّ وَ تَرْضٰى لَهْ

Allāhumma Salli 'alā Sayyidinā Muhammadin kamā tuhibbu wa tardā lah.

O Allāh, bless our Master Muhammad as You please and love for him.

اَللّٰهُمَّ صَلِّ عَلٰى رُوْحِ سَيِّدِنَا مُحَمَّدٍ فِى الْاَرْوَاحِ

Allāhumma Salli 'alā Rūhi Sayyidinā Muhammadin fi'l-arwāh.

O Allāh, bless the spirit of our Master Muhammad among all spirits.

اَللّٰهُمَّ صَلِّ عَلٰى جَسَدِ سَيِّدِنَا مُحَمَّدٍ فِى الْاَجْسَادِ

Allāhumma Salli 'alā jasadi Sayyidinā Muhammadin fi'l-ajsād.

O Allāh, bless the body of our Master Muhammad among all bodies.

اَللّٰهُمَّ صَلِّ عَلٰى قَبْرِ سَيِّدِنَا مُحَمَّدٍ فِى الْقُبُوْرِ

Allāhumma Salli 'alā Qabri Sayyidinā Muhammadin fi'l-qubūr.

O Allāh, bless the grave of our Master Muhammad among all graves.

صَلَّى اللهُ عَلَى سَيِّدِنَا وَ مَوْلَانَا مُحَمَّدٍ

Sall-Allāhu 'alā Sayyidinā wa Mawlānā Muhammad.

O Allāh, bless and send greetings of peace upon our Master and liege-lord Muhammad.

(2) This *du'ā* is a prayer for forgiveness that cleanses the heart, and safeguards the supplicant from all worldly, and spiritual ills. It should be read 100 times:[74]

اَللهُ لَا اِلٰهَ اِلَّا هُوَ الْحَىُّ الْقَيُّومُ اَللهُ لَا اِلٰهَ اِلَّا هُوَ
الرَّحْمٰنُ الرَّحِيْمُ اَللهُ لَا اِلٰهَ اِلَّا اَنْتَ سُبْحَانَكَ اِنِّىْ
كُنْتُ مِنَ الظَّالِمِيْنَ صَلِّ وَ سَلِّمْ وَ بَارِكْ اَبَدًا عَلَى
النَّبِىِّ الْأُمِّىِّ وَ آلِهِ وَ اَصْحَابِهِ اَجْمَعِيْنَ. اَللهُ اَللهُ اَللهُ لَا
اِلٰهَ اِلَّا اللهُ مُحَمَّدٌ رَّسُوْلُ اللهِ صَلَّى اللهُ تَعَالَى عَلَيْهِ وَ
سَلَّمَ. يَا غَوْثُ يَا غَوْثُ يَا غَوْثُ

Allāhu lā ilāha illa Huwal Hayyul Qayyūm. Allāhu lā ilāha illa Huwar Rahmānur Rahīm. Allāhu lā ilāha illa Anta Subhānaka innī kuntu minaz

---

[74] This formula combines two extremely potent supplications from the Holy Qur'ān (2:255 and 21:87) with *salawāt* upon the Prophet ﷺ. It ends with the recitation of the Divine Name, *Yā Ghawth* [O Succor]!

zālimīn. Salli wa sallim wa bārik abadan 'alan
Nabiyyil Ummiyyi wa ālihi wa ashābihi ajma'īn.
Allāhu   Allāhu   Allāhu   lā   ilāha   illAllāhu
Muhammadur Rasūlullāhi sall-Allāhu 'alayhi wa
Sallam. Yā Ghawth Yā Ghawth Yā Ghawth.[75]

Allāh, there is no god save Thee, the Living, the
Everlasting. Allāh, there is no god save Thee, the
Most Gracious, the Most Merciful. Allāh, there is no
god save Thee! Limitless art Thou in Thy glory.
Verily, I was mistaken. Blessings and peace be upon
the unlettered[76] Prophet and upon his Family and

---

[75] *Ghawth* is an Arabic word meaning: (1) A cry for aid or succor. (2)
Aid, help, succor; deliverance from adversity.

[76] Allāh Most High refers to His Messenger ﷺ (whom He gave
comprehensive knowledge of the unseen) as *ummī* in the Holy Qur'ān
(7:157-158). Our Prophet ﷺ also refers to himself as *ummī* in many
Ahādīth, including *Sahīh al-Bukhārī* (#1913), *Sahīh Muslim* (#2472),
Sunan Abū Dāwūd (#2319), *Sunan an-Nasā'ī al-Sughrā* (#2141) and
Musnad Ahmad, vol. 2/p. 44. Lexically, the meaning of *ummī* is someone
who does not read or write. But this attribute is one of the most
excellent virtues of the Beloved ﷺ, for he was taught by the All-
Knowing! *Ummī* also means the leader of those who could not read and
write, it also means the Prophet who was born in the Mother of all
Cities, Makkah the Ennobled (*Umm al-Qura*). For further discussion of
this topic, see Imām Rāghib al-Isfahanī's *al-Mufradat*, vol. 1/p. 29.
According to Imām Muhammad ibn Tahir al-Fattanī al-Gujratī (d.
986/1578), *ummī* also means those in a natural state of faith (*Majma'
Bihar al-Anwār*, vol. 1/p. 107). Imām Murtada al-Zabidī (d. 1205/1790)
states in his celebrated *Tāj al-'Arūs* that this was a true miracle of the
Beloved ﷺ, for despite being an *ummī*, he recited the entire Qur'ān
perfectly and conveyed the exact same wording of the Book without the
slightest variation. Although it is true that the Messenger of Allāh ﷺ

his Companions. Allāh! Allāh! Allāh! There is no
god save Thee. Muhammad is the Messenger of
Allāh, may blessings and peace be upon him. O
Succor! O Succor! O Succor!

Translator's Commentary: Prophet Yūnus صلى الله عليه وسلم offered a
portion of this prayer in the belly of an enormous fish:[77]
*"Allāh, there is no god save Thee! Limitless art Thou in Thy
glory. Verily, I was mistaken."* Prior to making this *du'ā*,
Prophet Yūnus صلى الله عليه وسلم had warned the people of Nineveh to
turn toward Allāh and repent, but they refused so he
boarded a ship and left them to their punishment. His
intention to board the ship was good, sound, and not an
"act of disobedience." He had not yet received the Divine
Command to stay, nor was it evident that the seeds of

---

was not taught to read or write by a human being; it is also true that he
did on occasion read and write as proven in many Ahādīth. The
following Hadīth related on the authority of al-Bara' ibn al-'Azib صلى الله عليه وسلم
should suffice: When the Treaty of Hudaybiyyah was being recorded,
Allāh's Messenger صلى الله عليه وسلم took the peace agreement from 'Alī صلى الله عليه وسلم and wrote,
"This is what Muhammad ibn 'Abdullāh has ratified that no weapon
will enter Makkah except in a sheath." This is a sound Hadīth narrated
by al-Bukhārī (#4251, 2699), and Imām Ahmad in his *Musnad*, vol. 4/p.
298. Hence, it is an irrefutable proof that the Beloved صلى الله عليه وسلم knew how to
read and write. How eloquently Imām al-Būsayrī صلى الله عليه وسلم put it in his *Qasīda
al-Burdah* [Ode of the Mantle], "It is sufficient for you as a miracle to be
blessed with such vast knowledge despite being an *ummī* in the period
of ignorance; what an immaculate orphan (indeed)!" And Allāh knows
best.
[77] Prophet Yūnus صلى الله عليه وسلم is also known as Dhul Nūn [Jonah of the Fish]
(Sūrah al-Anbiyā, 21:87).

91

Divine Oneness [*tawḥīd*] were about to sprout in the hearts of the people of Nineveh. Upon reading this supplication, Allāh Most High answered his prayer; the people of Nineveh entered into a state of submission [*Islam*] and accepted the prophethood of our liege-lord Yūnus ﷺ.

Unfortunately, this *du'ā* is commonly translated into English as "I have done evil" (Allāh forbid!) or "I have done wrong," which may lead English-speaking Muslims to erroneously conclude that Prophets are not preserved from sin. All Prophets are infallible [*mas'ūm*], because the One Who sent them and commanded us to follow them unconditionally has guided them (6:90). They incline infallibly toward goodness, which prevents them from evil.

Therefore, the best interpretation of the aforementioned verse is that Prophet Yūnus ﷺ was expressing personal humility in a state of complete submission to Allāh's will. He was also instructing us on how to make *du'ā*, as we (much like the people of Nineveh) are heedless, wrong-doers that need to repent and mend our evil ways. For further discussion of this topic, see Hadrat Muftī Muhammad Nizām ad-Dīn al-Misbahī's *'Ismat al-Anbiyā* [The Immunity of the Prophets from Error and Sin].

COMMENTARY ENDS

Supplications before Sleeping

(1) Read the Verse of the Throne [Āyat al-Kursī][78] before sleeping, as the supplicant and his family will remain under the protection of Allāh, the Sublime and Exalted, while they sleep. He will also be protected from theft and the mischief of Jinn.[79]

ٱللَّهُ لَآ إِلَـٰهَ إِلَّا هُوَ ٱلْحَىُّ ٱلْقَيُّومُ ۚ لَا تَأْخُذُهُۥ سِنَةٌ وَلَا نَوْمٌ ۚ لَّهُۥ مَا فِى ٱلسَّمَـٰوَٰتِ وَمَا فِى ٱلْأَرْضِ ۗ مَن ذَا ٱلَّذِى يَشْفَعُ عِندَهُۥٓ إِلَّا بِإِذْنِهِۦ ۚ يَعْلَمُ مَا بَيْنَ أَيْدِيهِمْ وَمَا خَلْفَهُمْ ۖ وَلَا يُحِيطُونَ بِشَىْءٍ مِّنْ عِلْمِهِۦٓ إِلَّا بِمَا شَآءَ ۚ وَسِعَ كُرْسِيُّهُ ٱلسَّمَـٰوَٰتِ وَٱلْأَرْضَ ۖ وَلَا يَـُٔودُهُۥ حِفْظُهُمَا ۚ وَهُوَ ٱلْعَلِىُّ ٱلْعَظِيمُ ﴿٢٥٥﴾

---

[78] Sūrah al-Baqarah, 2:255.

[79] Narrated from Abū Hurayrah ﷺ in *Sahīh al-Bukhārī* (#2311) as a *Ta'liq* [or, an excerpt of the Hadīth taken as the subject title], for an unabridged narration see *Sahīh al-Bukhārī* (#3275, 5010) and an-Nasā'ī in *'Amal al-Yawm wa'l Laylah* (#959). An-Nasā'ī relates an incident that occurred between Abū Hurayrah ﷺ and Shaytān, the accursed.

Allāhu lā ilāha 'illā huwa'l-Hayyul-Qayyūm. Lā ta'-
khuzuhū sina-tunw-wa lā nawm. Lahū
mā fissamāwāti wa mā fīl-'ard. Man-Dhālladhī
yashfa-'u 'indahū illā bī-idhnih. Ya-'lamu mā bayna
aydīhim wa mā khalfahum. Wa lā yu-hītūna bi-
shay-'im min 'il-mihī 'illā bimā shā'. Wa-si-'a
Kursiyyu-hus-Samāwā-ti wāl-'ard; wa lā ya-'ūdu-
hu hifzu-humā wa Huwal-'Aliyyul-'Azīm.

Allāh, there is no god but He, the Living, the
Everlasting. Slumber seizes Him not, neither sleep;
to Him belongs all that is in the heavens and the
earth. Who is there that shall intercede with Him
save by His leave? He knows what lies before them
and what is after them, and they comprehend not
anything of His knowledge save such as He wills.
His Throne comprises the heavens and earth; the
preserving of them oppresses Him not; He is the
All-High, the All-Glorious.

(2) Recite the glorification [*tasbīh*] given to Sayyidah
Fatima ﷺ by the Messenger of Allāh ﷺ: Say, "Subhān
Allāh" thirty-three times, "Alhamdulillāh" thirty-three
times, and "Allāhu Akbar" thirty-four times. The
supplicant will awake fresh and spiritually active.[80]

---

[80] *Sahīh al-Bukhārī*, vol. 2/p. 935 (#3113, 3705, 5361-5362, 6318); *Sahīh Muslim*, vol. 2/p. 351 (#2727); *Sunan Abū Dāwūd*, p. 350 (#5062-5063); *Jāmi' al-Tirmidhī*, vol. 2/p. 178 (#3405, 5062); *Musnad Ahmad*, vol. 1/p. 96; *Musnad al-Dārimī* (#2688).

(3) Recite Sūrah 1: al-Fātiha and the three Quls.[81]

بِسْمِ ٱللَّهِ ٱلرَّحْمَٰنِ ٱلرَّحِيمِ ۝ ٱلْحَمْدُ لِلَّهِ رَبِّ ٱلْعَٰلَمِينَ ۝ ٱلرَّحْمَٰنِ ٱلرَّحِيمِ ۝ مَٰلِكِ يَوْمِ ٱلدِّينِ ۝ إِيَّاكَ نَعْبُدُ وَإِيَّاكَ نَسْتَعِينُ ۝ ٱهْدِنَا ٱلصِّرَٰطَ ٱلْمُسْتَقِيمَ ۝ صِرَٰطَ ٱلَّذِينَ أَنْعَمْتَ عَلَيْهِمْ غَيْرِ ٱلْمَغْضُوبِ عَلَيْهِمْ وَلَا ٱلضَّآلِّينَ ۝

Bismillāhir-Rahmānir-Rahīm. 'Alhamdulillāhi Rabbil-'Ālamīn; 'Ar-Rahmānir-Rahīm; Māliki Yawmid-Dīn! 'Iyyāka na'-budu wa 'iyyāka nasta-'īn. 'Ihdinas-Sirātal-Mustaqīm—Sirātal-ladhīna 'an-'amta 'alay-him—Ghayril-maghdūbi 'alay-him wa lad-Dāllīn.

In the Name of Allāh, the Most Merciful, the Most Compassionate. Praise belongs to Allāh, the Cherisher and Sustainer of the worlds; the All-Merciful, the All-Compassionate, the Master of the Day of Judgment. Thee only do we worship; to Thee alone we pray for help. Guide us to the Straight Path, the Way of those Whom Thou hast

---

[81] *Sahīh al-Bukhārī*, (#5017, 5748, 6319); *Sahīh Muslim* (#2192); Imām Mālik's *Muwatta'*, vol. 2 (#942-943); *Jāmi' al-Tirmidhī* (#3399); *Sunan Abū Dāwūd* (#3902); *Musnad Ahmad*, vol. 6/pp. 116, 154; an-Nasā'ī in *'Amal al-Yawm wa'l Laylah* (#788, 1009); Ibn al-Sunnī in *'Amal al-Yawm wa'l Laylah* (#697).

blessed, not of those whose portion is wrath, nor those who go astray.

قُلْ هُوَ ٱللَّهُ أَحَدٌ ۝ ٱللَّهُ ٱلصَّمَدُ ۝ لَمْ يَلِدْ وَلَمْ يُولَدْ ۝ وَلَمْ يَكُن لَّهُ كُفُوًا أَحَدُ ۝

Qul Hu-wallāhu 'Ahad. Allāhus-Samad. Lam yalid, wa lam yūlad. Walam yakul-la-hu kufuwan 'ahad.

Say: "He is Allāh, the One and Only; Allāh, the Eternal, Absolute; He begetteth not, nor is He begotten; and there is none like unto Him."

قُلْ أَعُوذُ بِرَبِّ ٱلْفَلَقِ ۝ مِن شَرِّ مَا خَلَقَ ۝ وَمِن شَرِّ غَاسِقٍ إِذَا وَقَبَ ۝ وَمِن شَرِّ ٱلنَّفَّثَٰتِ فِي ٱلْعُقَدِ ۝ وَمِن شَرِّ حَاسِدٍ إِذَا حَسَدَ ۝

Qul 'a-ūdhu bi-Rabbil-Falaq. Min-sharri mā khalaq. Wa min-sharri ghāsiqin idhā waqab. Wa min-sharrin-Naffāthāti fīl-'uqad. Wa min-sharri ḥāsidin 'idhā ḥasad.

Say: "I seek refuge with the Lord of the Dawn. From the mischief of created things; from the mischief of darkness as it overspreads; and from the mischief of the envious one as he practices envy."

قُلْ أَعُوذُ بِرَبِّ ٱلنَّاسِ ۝ مَلِكِ ٱلنَّاسِ ۝ إِلَهِ ٱلنَّاسِ ۝
مِن شَرِّ ٱلْوَسْوَاسِ ٱلْخَنَّاسِ ۝ ٱلَّذِى يُوَسْوِسُ فِـ صُدُورِ
ٱلنَّاسِ ۝ مِنَ ٱلْجِنَّةِ وَٱلنَّاسِ ۝

Qul 'a-'ūdhu bi-Rabbin-Nās. Malikin-Nās, 'llāhin-
Nās. Min-sharril-Waswāsil-khan-Nās, 'Alladhī
yuwas-wisu fī sudūrin-Nās, Minal-Jinnati wan-
Nās.

Say: "I seek refuge with the Lord and Cherisher of
men, the King of men, the God of men, from the
mischief of him, who breathes temptations into the
minds of men, who whispers evil thoughts to the
hearts of men, from among the Jinns and men."

(4) Recite the first five verses of Sūrah 2: al-Baqarah till "it
is these who will prosper" [*al-muflihūn*].[82]

---

[82] Our Prophet ﷺ said, "Whoever recites four verses from the first part
of Sūrah al-Baqarah (2:1-4), the Verse of the Throne (2:255), the two
verses that follow the Verse of the Throne (2:256-258), and the last three
verses of Sūrah al Baqarah (2:284-286), Shaytān will never come near
him or the members of his family on the day of his recital, and what he
despises will not approach him or the members of his family; and these
veres are never recited over a madman without him gaining
consciousness." Related by ad-Dārimī in his *Sunan* (#3249/A), Ibn
Hibbān, and at-Tabarānī. 'Abdullāh ibn Mas'ūd ﷺ said, "Whoever
recited ten verses from al-Baqarah during the night, Shaytān shall not

الٓمٓ ۞ ذَٰلِكَ ٱلْكِتَـٰبُ لَا رَيْبَ ۛ فِيهِ ۛ هُدًى لِّلْمُتَّقِينَ ۞
ٱلَّذِينَ يُؤْمِنُونَ بِٱلْغَيْبِ وَيُقِيمُونَ ٱلصَّلَوٰةَ وَمِمَّا رَزَقْنَـٰهُمْ يُنفِقُونَ
۞ وَٱلَّذِينَ يُؤْمِنُونَ بِمَا أُنزِلَ إِلَيْكَ وَمَا أُنزِلَ مِن قَبْلِكَ وَبِٱلْأَخِرَةِ
هُمْ يُوقِنُونَ ۞ أُوْلَـٰئِكَ عَلَىٰ هُدًى مِّن رَّبِّهِمْ ۖ وَأُوْلَـٰئِكَ هُمُ
ٱلْمُفْلِحُونَ ۞

Alif Lām Mīm. Dhālikal-Kitābu lā rayba fīh. Hudal-lil-Muttaqīn; 'Alladhīna yu'-minūna bil-Ghaybi wa yuqīmūnas-Salāha wa mimmā razaqnāhum yunfiqūn; Walladhīna yu'-minūna bimā 'unzila 'ilayka wa mā 'unzila min-qablik, wa bil-'Ākhirati hum yūqinūn. 'Ulā-'ika 'alā Hudammir-Rabbihim wa 'ulā-'ika humul-Muflihūn.

Alif Lām Mīm. This is the Book free of doubt and involution, a guidance for those who preserve themselves from evil and follow the Straight Path, who believe in the unseen and are steadfast in prayer, and spend out of what We have provided for them; who believe in what has been revealed to

---

have access to that house at the night till the reciter wakes in the morning. These ten verses are: the first four verses of the Sūrah (2:1-4), followed by the Verse of the Throne (2:255), the two verses after the Verse of the Throne (2:256-258), and the last three verses of the Sūrah (2:284-286)." Narrated by ad-Dārimī in his *Sunan* (#3248/A).

you [O beloved Messenger ﷺ] and what was revealed to those before you, and are certain of the Hereafter. They have found the guidance of their Lord and will be successful.

(5) Recite the second verse of "The Messenger believes..." [*Amana 'r-Rasūlu*, 2:285-286] in Sūrah 2: al-Baqarah. The benefits of this supplication [*du'ā*] are too numerous to mention.[83]

لَا يُكَلِّفُ ٱللَّهُ نَفْسًا إِلَّا وُسْعَهَا ۚ لَهَا مَا كَسَبَتْ وَعَلَيْهَا مَا ٱكْتَسَبَتْ ۗ

رَبَّنَا لَا تُؤَاخِذْنَا إِن نَّسِينَا أَوْ أَخْطَأْنَا ۚ رَبَّنَا وَلَا تَحْمِلْ عَلَيْنَا

إِصْرًا كَمَا حَمَلْتَهُۥ عَلَى ٱلَّذِينَ مِن قَبْلِنَا ۚ رَبَّنَا وَلَا تُحَمِّلْنَا مَا

لَا طَاقَةَ لَنَا بِهِۦ ۖ وَٱعْفُ عَنَّا وَٱغْفِرْ لَنَا وَٱرْحَمْنَا ۚ أَنتَ مَوْلَىٰنَا

فَٱنصُرْنَا عَلَى ٱلْقَوْمِ ٱلْكَٰفِرِينَ ﴿٢٨٦﴾

---

[83] Abū Mas'ūd 'Uqbah ibn 'Amr al-Anṣārī al-Badrī ﷺ relates that the Messenger of Allāh ﷺ said: "Whosoever recites the last two verses of Sūrah al-Baqarah during the night, they shall suffice him." Narrated in *Ṣaḥīḥ al-Bukhārī* (#4008, 5008-5009, 5040, 5051); *Ṣaḥīḥ Muslim* (#808); *Jāmi' al-Tirmidhī* (#2884); *Sunan Abū Dāwūd* (#1397); *Sunan Ibn Mājah* (#1369); *Musnad Aḥmad*, vol. 4/pp. 118, 121-122; ad-Dārimī in his *Sunan* (#1495, 3391); and an-Nasā'ī in *'Amal al-Yawm wa'l Laylah* (#718-721). According to the Ḥadīth commentators "suffice him" means from all calamities throughout the night. And Allāh knows best.

Lā yukalli-fullāhu naf-san 'illā wus-'ahā. Lahā mā kasabat wa 'alay-hā mak-tasabat. Rabbanā lā tu-'ā-khidhnā 'in-nasīnā 'aw 'akhta'-nā. Rabbanā wa lā tahmil 'alay-nā 'is-ran kamā hamal-ta-hū 'alal-ladhīna min qablinā. Rabbanā wa lā tuhammil-nā mā lā tāqata lanā bih. Wa'-fu 'annā, wagh-fir lanā, war-ham-nā. 'Anta Mawlānā fan-surnā 'alal qawmil-Kāfirīn.

On no soul doth Allāh place a burden greater than it can bear. It gets every good that it earns, and it suffers every ill that it earns. (Pray:) "Our Lord! Condemn us not if we forget or fall into error. Our Lord! Lay not on us a burden like that which Thou didst lay on those before us. Our Lord! Lay not on us a burden greater than we have strength to bear. Blot out our sins, and grant us forgiveness, have mercy on us. Thou art our Protector; help us against those who stand against faith."

(6) Recite the last four verses of Sūrah 18: al-Kahf.[84]

---

[84] Abū 'd-Dardā' ❀ relates that the noble Prophet ❀ said, "Whoever memorizes the first ten verses of Sūrah al-Kahf will be protected from the Anti-Christ [*Dajjāl*]." Narrated by Muslim, Abū Dāwūd, an-Nasā'ī, and others; with Muslim's wording. In another narration, Muslim and Abū Dāwūd specifically mention ten verses "from the end of Sūrah al-Kahf." At-Tirmidhī related it with the words: "Whoever recites three verses from the beginning of al-Kahf will be protected from the tribulations of the Dajjāl." By way of comparison, at-Tabarānī's version reads: "Whoever recites the last ten verses of Sūrah al-Kahf, and then the Dajjāl reveals himself [during the reciter's lifetime]; he will have no

إِنَّ ٱلَّذِينَ ءَامَنُواْ وَعَمِلُواْ ٱلصَّٰلِحَٰتِ كَانَتْ لَهُمْ جَنَّٰتُ ٱلْفِرْدَوْسِ نُزُلاً ۝ خَٰلِدِينَ فِيهَا لَا يَبْغُونَ عَنْهَا حِوَلاً ۝ قُل لَّوْ كَانَ ٱلْبَحْرُ مِدَادًا لِّكَلِمَٰتِ رَبِّى لَنَفِدَ ٱلْبَحْرُ قَبْلَ أَن تَنفَدَ كَلِمَٰتُ رَبِّى وَلَوْ جِئْنَا بِمِثْلِهِۦ مَدَدًا ۝ قُلْ إِنَّمَآ أَنَا۠ بَشَرٌ مِّثْلُكُمْ يُوحَىٰ إِلَىَّ أَنَّمَآ إِلَٰهُكُمْ إِلَٰهٌ وَٰحِدٌ فَمَن كَانَ يَرْجُواْ لِقَآءَ رَبِّهِۦ فَلْيَعْمَلْ عَمَلاً صَٰلِحًا وَلَا يُشْرِكْ بِعِبَادَةِ رَبِّهِۦٓ أَحَدًۢا ۝

'Innalladhīna 'āmanū wa 'amilus-sālihāti kānat lahum Jannātul-Firdawsi nu-zulā, Khālidīna fīhā lā yabghūna 'anhā hiwalā. Qul-law kānal-bahru midādal-li-Kalimāti Rabbī lanafidal-bahru qabla 'an-tan-fada Kalimātu Rabbī wa law ji'-nā bi-mithlihī madadā. Qul 'innamā 'ana bashar[85]um-mithlukum yūhā 'ilayya 'annamā Ilāhukum Ilāhunw-Wāhid: faman kāna yarjū Liqā-'a Rabbihī fal-ya'-mal 'amalan sālihanw wa lā yushrik bi-'ibādati Rabbihī 'ahadā.

But those who believe, and do deeds of righteousness—Gardens of Paradise shall be their

---

influence over him." For further discussion of this topic, see al-Mundhirī's *al-Targhib wal Tarhib* (#2172-2173).

[85] *Bashar* is an Arabic word meaning: (1) Outer skin. (2) Countenance, face, appearance. (3) Human being, mortal.

hospitality, therein to dwell forever, desiring no removal out of them. Say [O beloved Prophet ﷺ]: "Though the sea became ink for the Words of my Lord, verily the sea would be used up before the Words of my Lord were exhausted, even though We brought the like thereof to replenish it." Say: "I am only a mortal [*bashar*] like you, but I receive revelation.[86] And whoever hopeth for the meeting with his Lord should do what is right, and associate none as a partner in the worship of his Lord."

(7) **Nota Bene:** Remember to read the three Quls before sleeping. The supplicant should blow into his hands and

---

[86] Our Prophet ﷺ is a mirror reflecting Allāh's beauty. On one side of this mirror, the Messenger of Allāh ﷺ is light. But on the opposite side, he has been given the covering of a man [*bashar*]. Thus, through these diverse natures he becomes a complete mirror. *Āyat* 18:110 refers to the latter, while verse 5:15 affirms the former: *There has come to you a Light [Nūr] from Allāh, and a Manifest Book (Tafsīr Nūr-ul-Irfān, vol. 2/pp. 961-962).* Classical Qur'ānic exegetes like Jalāl ad-Dīn al-Suyūtī in his *Tafsīr al-Jalālayn*, Ibn Jarīr at-Tabarī in his *Jāmi' al-Bayan*, Fakhr al-Rāzī in his *al-Tafsīr al-Kabīr*, al-Baghawī in his *Ma'ālam al-Tanzīl*, and al-Qurtubī in his *Ahkām al-Qur'ān* concur that the "Light" [*Nūr*] is Muhammad ﷺ, and the "Manifest Book" is the inimitable Qur'ān. In this regard Imām al-Būsayrī provides a beautiful parable: "Muhammad ﷺ is a human being, but not like humankind; for he is like a ruby among stones" (*Qasīda al-Burdah*). Let us recapitulate once again that in *āyat* 18:110, the Messenger of Allāh ﷺ declared his mortality as an expression of his dignity and humility, and to destroy any claim to a nature other than human—i.e., god or angel—that might be attributed to him, whilst affirming his unique station and rank as *one who is divinely inspired* with truth and guidance, light and radiance!

pass his hands over his entire body.[87] This will also protect him against the whisperings of Shaytān, the accursed. [The author made it a point to repeat this injunction, thus reiterating its importance for our spiritual well-being, and reminding us not to overlook it. May Allāh Most High bless us with *istiqāmah*[88] in fulfilling this Sunnah of the Messenger of Allāh 鬱, āmīn.]

Finally, the supplicant should recite Sūrah 109: al-Kāfirūn and then try to sleep. If he engages in conversation thereafter, he may do so. However, he must read Sūrah 109: al-Kāfirūn again before going to sleep.[89] [This Chapter of the Holy Qur'ān protects the supplicant from associating partners with Allāh Most Pure.]

---

[87] It has been narrated in *Sahīh al-Bukhārī* and *Sahīh Muslim* from 'Ā'isha 靠 that, "When the Prophet 鬱 would take his place for resting, he used to blow into his hands and recite the three Quls and pass and wipe his hands over the body." Related by Imām an-Nawawī in his *al-Adhkār*, p. 122.

[88] *Istiqāmah*: steadfastness.

[89] Narrated on the authority of Nawfal al-Ashja'ī 靠 and 'Abdullāh ibn 'Abbās 靠. The Hadīth of Nawfal 靠 is related by Abū Dāwūd (#5055), at-Tirmidhī (#3400-3401), Imām Ahmad in his *Musnad*, vol. 1/p. 456, ad-Dārimī (#3430), and an-Nasā'ī in his *'Amal al-Yawm wa'l Laylah* (#801-804). Ibn Hibbān said it is authentic and sound (#2363), as did al-Hākim in his *al-Mustadrak*, vol. 2/p. 538.

قُلْ يَـٰٓأَيُّهَا ٱلْكَـٰفِرُونَ ۝ لَآ أَعْبُدُ مَا تَعْبُدُونَ ۝ وَلَآ أَنتُمْ

عَـٰبِدُونَ مَآ أَعْبُدُ ۝ وَلَآ أَنَا۠ عَابِدٌ مَّا عَبَدتُّمْ ۝ وَلَآ أَنتُمْ

عَـٰبِدُونَ مَآ أَعْبُدُ ۝ لَكُمْ دِينُكُمْ وَلِىَ دِينِ ۝

Qul yā-'ayyuhal-Kāfirūn! Lā 'a'-budu mā ta'-bu-
dūn, Wa lā 'antum 'ābidūna mā 'a'-bud. Wa lā 'ana
'ābidum-mā 'aba(d)tum, Wa lā 'antum 'ābidūna mā
'a'-bud. Lakum Dīnukum wa li-ya Dīn!

Say: "O disbelievers! I do not worship what you
worship. Nor do you worship who I worship. Nor
will I worship what you worship. Nor will you
worship who I worship. For you is your religion,
and for me is my religion."

The Night Vigil Prayer

The night vigil prayer [*Salāh at-Tahajjud*] is said upon waking from sleep; it is performed after the 'Ishā prayer [and before the start of Fajr]. The supplicant should perform at least two cycles [*raka'āt*] of prayer. However, the Sunnah is to perform eight cycles [*raka'āt*]. He should also recite as much of the Holy Qur'ān as possible within these cycles [*raka'āt*]. If he does not know any long Chapters, then he may read Sūrah 112: al-Ikhlās three times in each cycle, by doing so he will gain the reward of reading the entire Qur'ān.

Translator's Commentary: The following Ahādīth testify to the greatness of this prayer in the sight of Allāh the Exatled. Abū Hurayrah ؓ relates that the Messenger of Allāh ﷺ said: "The most virtuous fasting after the fasting of Ramadan is fasting in the month of Muharram, and the most virtuous prayer after the obligatory prayers is the night prayer."[90] Similarly Abū Hurayrah ؓ reports that the Holy Prophet ﷺ said: "If you get up for night prayer and awaken your wife so that both of you pray two short

---

[90] *Jāmi' al-Tirmidhī*, vol. 1/p. 99.

cycles, then you shall be counted among the oft-remembering men and women [*al-dhākirīn/al-dhākirāt⁹¹*]."⁹²

Abū Hurayrah ﷺ narrates that the Messenger of Allāh ﷺ said, "Our Lord descends⁹³ every night to the lowest heaven when one-third of the latter part of the night is left, and says: 'Who supplicates unto Me so that I may answer him? Who asks forgiveness from Me so that I may forgive him?' [The call continues] until the break of dawn."⁹⁴

According to a traditional report that has been handed down to us from 'Amr ibn al-'Ās ﷺ, the Messenger of Allāh ﷺ once said: "The Most beloved of prayers in the sight of Allāh is the prayer of [Prophet] Dāwūd ﷺ and most beloved of all fasts is the fast of [Prophet] Dāwūd ﷺ. He would sleep half the night and would stand [in prayer] for a third of it, and then he would sleep in the sixth portion of the night. He made it his practice to fast every other day throughout the entire year."⁹⁵

'Abdullāh ibn Salam ﷺ reports that: "When the Messenger of Allāh ﷺ blessed the city of Madinah with his arrival, people flocked to see him and they shouted: 'The Messenger of Allāh ﷺ has arrived!' I also came out to be present amongst those visiting the Messenger ﷺ. When I

---

⁹¹ *Al-dhākirīn/al-dhākirāt:* those who remember Allāh Almighty at all times.

⁹² Reported by Ibn Mājah in his *Sunan*.

⁹³ The word "descends" is meant figuratively, as Allāh Almighty has no modality. He is transcendent beyond limits, ends, supports, components, and the six directions do not contain Him as they do created things.

⁹⁴ Narrated by Muslim in his *Saḥīḥ*.

⁹⁵ Related by al-Bukhārī in his *Saḥīḥ*.

glanced at his radiant face, I immediately knew that his face was not that of a liar. The first noble utterance [*Hadīth Sharīf*] I heard from him was: 'O people! Spread the greeting of peace [*salām*], feed others, maintain family ties, and pray at night when others sleep, and you will enter heaven safely.'"[96]

Abū Sa'īd al-Khudrī ﷺ is reported as having said: "A person heard someone[97] recite *Say: He is Allāh, the One and Only* [Sūrah 112: al-Ikhlās] over and over again. This person then came to the Messenger of Allāh ﷺ and told him about what he had overheard. Allāh's Messenger ﷺ said, 'By the One in Whose hand[98] is my soul! Verily, this Sūrah is a third of the Holy Qur'ān.'"[99]

COMMENTARY ENDS

---

[96] Reported by at-Tirmidhi (#849), ad-Dārimī in his *Sunan*, and Mullā 'Alī al-Qārī in his *Mishkāt al-Masābīh* (#1907).

[97] Qatada ibn Nu'mān ﷺ

[98] The "hand" of Allāh possibly alludes to His *control* over the Prophet's soul ﷺ, though we leave its final meaning to Allāh. Muslims must guard against anthropomorphic literalism when interpreting this Hadīth, as the Exalted has informed us that: *Naught is as His likeness* (42:11).

[99] Narrated in *Sahīh al-Bukhārī*, vol. 2/ p. 750 (#4726); *Sunan Abū Dāwūd*, vol. 1/p. 206 (#1461); and *Sunan an-Nasā'ī* (#995). Imām Badr al-Dīn al-'Aynī in his commentary on this Hadīth has mentioned numerous insights about the Prophet's declaration ﷺ concerning the exalted status of Sūrah al-Ikhlās. One of these insights is that the entire content of the Qur'ān can be divided into three subject categories: (1) incidents [*al-Waqi'at*], (2) rulings [*al-Ahkam*], and (3) Divine Attributes [*al-Sifat*]. Sūrah al-Ikhlās covers the latter and hence, it is a third of the Holy Qur'ān (*'Umdat al-Qārī*, vol. 20/p. 33). And Allāh knows best.

Qur'ānic Recitation

The Friends of Allāh, who attain integral human perfection [al-Awlīyā al-Kāmilīn], have mentioned that no litany [wazīfah] is better than that of the continuous recitation of the Holy Qur'ān.[100] They have given us a seven day course for the khatm[101] of the Qur'ān, which has been divided [conveniently] according to the days of the week:

- ❖ **Friday** recite Sūrah 1: al-Fātiha until the end of Sūrah 5: al-Māīdah.
- ❖ **Saturday** read Sūrah 6: al-An'ām until the end of Sūrah 9: at-Tawba.
- ❖ **Sunday** recite Sūrah 10: Yūnus until the end of Sūrah 19: Maryam.
- ❖ **Monday** read Sūrah 20: Tā Hā until the end of Sūrah 28: al-Qasas.

---

[100] Mullā 'Alī al-Qārī ﷺ in his *Fayd al-Mu'īn 'alā Jam'il-Arba'īn fī Fadl al-Qur'ān al-Mubīn* relates a *marfū'* narration from Ibn Umar ﷺ, who said: "Recite the Qur'ān every month; recite it every twenty nights; recite it every ten; recite it every seven, but do not read more than this." This Hadīth is also narrated by al-Bukhārī, Muslim, and Abū Dāwūd.

[101] *Khatm*: literally "to seal," to conclude, close, finish, or complete the recitation of the Book of Allāh.

❖ **Tuesday** recite Sūrah 29: al-Ankabūt until the end of Sūrah 38: Sād.
❖ **Wednesday** read Sūrah 39: az-Zumar until the end of Sūrah 55: ar-Rahmān.
❖ **Thursday** recite Sūrah 56: al-Wāqi'ah until the end of Sūrah 114: an-Nās.

The reciter should try his level best to implement this seven day course for completing the Holy Qur'ān. He may not be able to accomplish this task initially. But he should realize that if he perseveres, then it will be incumbent upon the Sufi saints [awlīyā] to see that he [ultimately] succeeds through their blessings.

Translator's Commentary: Bear in mind that A'lāhadrat ﷺ himself notes that this task may be impossible to accomplish at first, but he stresses that the key to our success is faith in the Friends of Allāh and perseverance. Our resolve should not weaken, nor should our current level of recitation diminish. May Allāh the Exalted grant us enabling success [tawfīq] and steadfastness [istiqāmah] in performing this good deed, āmīn.

COMMENTARY ENDS

Supplications for Success

By al-Muftī al-A'zam Shaykh Mustafā Ridā Khān ⚘

SUPPLICATIONS AFTER THE RITUAL PRAYER

(1) Recite the Verse of the Throne [*Āyat al-Kursī*] after each ritual prayer [*salāh*].

(2) Al-Ghawth al-A'zam Sultān al-Awlīyā' Sayyidunā 'sh-Shaykh Muhyi'd-Dīn 'Abd al-Qādir al-Jīlānī al-Hasanī al-Husaynī ⚘ has commanded his disciples [*murīds*] and followers to recite *Panj Ganj al-Qādiriyyah* ("The Five Treasures of Shaykh 'Abd al-Qādir ⚘") 100 times every day, after each ritual prayer [*salāh*].[102] Most of the adherents of the Qādirī Tarīqah assiduously follow this litany [*wazīfah*]:

1. After the **Fajr** prayer recite *Yā 'Azīzu Yā Allāh* (O All-Mighty One! O Allāh!)
2. After the **Zuhr** prayer recite *Yā Karīmu Yā Allāh* (O Ever-Generous One! O Allāh!)

---

[102] These supplications were recited by al-Ghawth al-A'zam ⚘ himself. See al-Maktabah al-Azhariyyah's publication *al-Fuyūdat al-Rabbāniyyah fī'l Awrād al-Qādiriyyah* (Cairo).

3. After the **'Asr** prayer recite *Yā Jabbāru Yā Allāh* (O All-Compelling One! O Allāh!)
4. After the **Maghrib** prayer recite *Yā Sattāru Yā Allāh* (O Veiler of faults! O Allāh!)
5. After the **'Ishā** prayer recite *Yā Ghaffāru Yā Allāh* (O Pardoning One! O Allāh!)

The noble grandson of Imām Ahmad Ridā Khān ﷺ, al-Mufassir al-A'zam Shaykh Ibrāhīm Ridā Khān "Jīlānī Miyā" ﷺ commented on this litany in *Fadā'il Durūd Sharīf:*[103]

"Men of spiritual insight know well the wisdom that lies behind specifying a particular Divine Name after every ritual prayer [*salāh*].

Yā 'Azīz has been enjoined upon us after the Fajr prayer, as the day is about to commence. Inevitably, the supplicant will come across both friend and foe throughout the day. In addition to this, he will be preoccupied with fulfilling his worldly duties, too. *Yā 'Azīz* means 'O All-Mighty One!' The reciter of this Divine Name will manifest the attribute of might, strength, and power by which he will always maintain the upper-hand in critical situations, and even when he finds himself in a predicament he shall gain honor and respect. Verily, he who remembers Allāh often remains

---

[103] *Fadā'il Durūd Sharīf*, pp. 100-103.

honored and overcomes his antagonists by the omnipotence of the Almighty.

Yā Karīm (O Ever-Generous One!) is recited after the Zuhr prayer in accordance with the Laws of Nature. For plants open their buds early in the evening and spread their fragrance throughout the night. Then they wither and droop during the afternoon and thereafter the seed germinates within the plant and it ripens. [Afternoon is the time when the] seal of sustenance is stamped on each seed within that plant. Hence, there is a great hope of having affluence in the supplicant's sustenance by reciting *Yā Karīm* at that time.

Yā Jabbār is recited at the time of 'Asr. This Name is from the Names of Majesty [*Asma' Jalaliyyah*]; it is a very powerful Attribute of Allāh Most High. [According to a Hadīth in *Sahīh Muslim*] Shaytān lays his throne on the surface of the sea with great pomp and show and calls a meeting at the time of 'Asr. All his minions congregate to devise innumerable traps to destroy mankind. [Just as there are angels that accompany us,] every individual has his own devil, who attends this 'conference.' Our devils are given guidance on how they can incline us toward evil and ruin our lives. Ultimately, Shaytān's minions agree to undertake certain tasks saying, 'I'll do this, and you do that.'[104] Hence, 'Asr is the most appropriate time to invoke

---

[104] *Sahīh Muslim* (#2813).

Allāh with His Name of Power, *Yā Jabbār* (O All-Compelling One!) so that His anger and wrath manifest upon these demonic creatures, and He grants us protection from their mischief by thwarting their plots and ruining their tricks.

Yā Sattār (O Veiler of faults!) is recited after the Maghrib prayer when the redness on the horizon disappears and complete darkness occurs. This is a time when animals of prey such as snakes, scorpions, thieves, robbers, and other beings [from the unseen realm] come out to inflict harm. Calamities and catastrophes swirl around during the night. Reciting *Yā Sattāru* at this time safeguards the reciter from all such calamities, and he will remain in the protection of Allāh Most High. Furthermore, mankind tends to commit sin more often at night than at any other time. That is why we should seek refuge in the mercy of Allāh and in His Attribute of Veiling at the beginning of the night so that we do not fall into a pit of sin throughout the night.

Yā Ghaffār (O Pardoning One!) is a Name of Allāh Most High that prevents the 'honorable recorders' [*Kirāman Katibīn*][105] from cataloguing the sins we committed during the day. These major and minor sins are punishable in the fire. If, however,

---

[105] *Kirāman Katibīn*: the "honorable recorders" are two angels that sit on a person's right and left shoulders; they record his good and bad deeds, respectively. There is reference to these angels in the Glorious Qur'ān (82:10-11).

the person repents before sleeping [e.g., by uttering: '*Yā Ghaffār* (O Pardoning One!)'] in the dark of the night, then Allāh will erase his sins that were recorded in his Book of Deeds. In light of this wisdom, we have been admonished to remain silent and refrain from worldly conversation after the 'Ishā prayer.

Besides, performing the ritual prayer [*salāh*] after a third of the night has elapsed is recommended, which means the supplicant can recite this litany [*wazīfah*] after completing the prayer and promptly go to bed. As a result [of adhering to this prophetic recommendation], he will be safeguarded from unworthy speech — backbiting, slander, lying, etc. and so forth. Thus, no transgression is recorded in his Book of Deeds."

SUPPLICATIONS AFTER THE FAJR & MAGHRIB PRAYERS

After the Fajr prayer, but before sunrise, and also after the Maghrib prayer recite the following supplications ten times:

❖ *Hasbiy Allāhu lā ilāha illa Huwa alayhi tawakkaltu wa Huwa Rabbul 'Arshil 'Adhīm* ["Allāh is Sufficient for me; and there is no one worthy of worship save Him.

Upon Him I put my trust, and He is the Lord of the Exalted Throne."][106]

❖ *Rabbi innī massaniyad durru wa anta Arhamur Rahimīn* ["O my Lord! Indeed distress has seized me, but You are the Most Merciful of those who show mercy."][107]

❖ *Rabbi inna maghlūbun fantasir* ["O my Lord! Indeed I have been overcome so assist me."][108]

❖ *Sa-yuhzamul jam'u wa yuwallunad dubur* ["Their multitude will be put to flight and they will show their backs."][109]

❖ *Allāhumma inna naj'aluka fi nuhūrihim wa na'ūdhubika min shurūrihim* ["O Allāh! Indeed we place You before our enemies and we seek refuge in You from their evil."][110]

After the Fajr prayer, but before sunrise, and also after the Maghrib prayer recite the following supplications three times:

❖ *Bismillāhil ladhi lā yadurru ma'asmihi shay'un fil-Ardi wa lā fis-Sama'i wa Huwas Samī'ul 'Alīm* ["In the Name of Allāh; with His name, nothing whatsoever on earth or heaven can inflict any harm; He is All-Hearing and All-Knowing."]

---

[106] Related by Abū Dāwūd ﷺ and Ibn al-Sunnī ﷺ.
[107] Sūrah al-Anbiyā, 21:83.
[108] Sūrah al-Qamar, 54:10.
[109] Sūrah al-Qamar, 54:45.
[110] Narrated by Abū Dāwūd ﷺ and al-Hākim ﷺ.

❖ *Rabbana lā taqtulnā bi-ghadabika wa lā tuhliknā bi-'adhābika wa 'āfinā qabla dhālik innaka antas samī'ul 'alīm* ["O Lord, do not slay us out of Your anger, and do not destroy us through Your punishment, but grant us protection before harm befalls us! Verily, You are the All-Hearing, the All-Knowing."][111]

❖ *Subhān Allāhi wa bi-hamdihi lā Quwwata illa billāh Masha-Allāh kana wa ma lam yasha' lam yakun a'lamu ann-Allāh 'alā kulli shay'in Qadīr wa ann-Allāhu qad Ahāta bi-kulli shay'in 'Ilma* ["Glory be to Allāh; all praise belongs to Him alone. There is no might except from Allāh. Whatever Allāh wills happens, whatever He does not will does not happen. I affirm my belief that surely Allāh has power over everything and verily He has encompassed everything through His knowledge."]

❖ *A'ūdhu bi-kalimatillahit tammati min sharri ma khalaq* ["I seek refuge in the perfect words of Allāh from the evil of what has been created."]

❖ *Yā Hafidhu, Yā Hāfidhu, Yā Raqību, Yā Wakīlu, Yā Salāmu, Yā Kabīru, Yā Muhītu* ["O Protector! O Guardian! O Watchful One! O Trustee! O Source of Peace! O Supremely Great One! O All-Encompassing One!"]

❖ *Inna Rabbi 'alā kulli shay'in hafidh. Fallahu khayrun hāfidhaw wa huwa Arhamur Rahimīn wa Allāhu muhītum bil-kafirīn. Wallahu min warā'ihin muhīt bal huwa*

---

[111] Shaykh 'Abd al-Qādir ❖ in his *Sufficient Provisions for Seekers of the Path of Truth* recommends reciting the aforementioned supplication when a person hears the crash of thunder and sees flashes of lightning (vol. 1/p. 385).

Qur'ānum majīdun fī lawhim mahfudh ["Verily, my Lord keeps watch over all things.[112] Why, Allāh is the best guardian, and He is the Most Merciful of all.[113] Nay, but the disbelievers still cry lies, and Allāh is behind them, encompassing. This is indeed a glorious Qur'ān, in a guarded Tablet."][114]

❖ *Wash-Shamsa wal-Qamara wan-Nujūma Musakh-kharatim bi-Amrihi 'alā lahul Khalqu wal-Amru tabarak Allāhu Rabbul 'Alāmīn* ["He created the sun, the moon, and the stars, (all) governed by laws under His command. Is it not His to create and to govern? Blessed be Allāh, the Cherisher and Sustainer of the worlds!"][115]

A SUPPLICATION FOR THE UMMAH

(1) The supplicant should ask Allāh the Exalted to protect the Community of Sayyidunā Muhammad ﷺ by reciting Sūrah 1: al-Fātiha 100 times anytime in the morning or the evening, as a member of this Community par excellence he is naturally included in the prayer. When reciting Sūrah al-Fātiha, it is important to join the *mīm* of *ar-Rahīm* with the *lām* of *Alhamdu* like this *Bismi'llahi'r-Rahmani'r Rahīmil-Hamdu*.

Another method is to recite Sūrah al-Fātiha thirty times after the Fajr prayer, twenty-five times after the Zuhr prayer, twenty times after the 'Asr prayer, five times after

---

[112] Sūrah Hūd, 11:57.
[113] Sūrah Yūsuf, 12:64.
[114] Sūrah al-Burūj, 85:20-22.
[115] Sūrah al-A'rāf, 7:54.

the Maghrib prayer, and ten times after the 'Ishā prayer. Whenever it is recited, the supplicant should make *du'ā* for the fulfillment of their permissible aims and objectives.

Those who do not have much time may say Sūrah al-Fātiha seven times after each prayer. Then they should offer their supplication. Those who do not even have time for this, should recite it seven times in the morning and seven times in the evening.

SUPPLICATIONS BEFORE SLEEPING

(1) Before sleeping recite Sūrah 1: al-Fātiha, the Verse of the Throne [*Āyat al-Kursī*], and the three Quls once with the exception of Sūrah 112: al-Ikhlās, which should be recited three times.

(2) When reciting Sūrah al-Fātiha, sleep with the intention of protection: First send blessings upon the Prophet ﷺ [*durūd sharīf*] three times, then utter the whole phrase, *Bismi'llahi'r-Rahmani'r Rahīmil-Hamdu*, by joining the *mīm* of *ar-Rahīm* with the *lām* of *Alhamdu*. Conclude the recitation of Sūrah al-Fātiha by sending blessings and salutations upon the Messenger of Allāh ﷺ three times.

Salutations upon the Chosen One ﷺ

[The author concludes this irreplaceable handbook with] *Durūd al-Radawiyya* ("Salutations of Imām Ahmad Ridā" upon the Messenger of Allāh ﷺ):

صَلَّى اللهُ عَلَى النَّبِيِّ الْأُمِّيِّ وَ آلِمِ صَلَّى اللهُ عَلَيْهِ وَ
سَلَّمَ صَلَا ةً وَّ سَلَامًا عَلَيْكَ يَا رَسُوْلَ اللهِ

Sall-Allāhu 'alan-Nabiyyil Ummiyyi wa Ālihi. Sall-Allāhu 'alayhi wa sallam. Salāhaw wa Salāman 'alayka yā Rasūl Allāh

May Allāh's blessings and greetings of peace be upon the unlettered Prophet, and upon his Family. May Allāh's blessings and greetings of peace be upon him. Peace and blessings be upon you, O Messenger of Allāh!"

After the Friday prayer [*jumu'ah salāh*] recite the above *durūd sharīf* 100 times (in a congregation if possible). Be sure to face the direction of the illumined city of Madinah and send prayers and salutations upon the Prophet ﷺ with the highest regard and utmost respect. Where the Friday prayer [*jumu'ah salāh*] is not established, then this *durūd sharīf* can be recited after the Fajr prayer on Friday, or after the Zuhr and 'Asr prayers. The supplicant may recite this formula after the ritual prayer wherever he is, even if he is on his own. Likewise, women should read this *durūd sharīf* in their homes after completing the ritual prayer on Friday in a similar manner.

There are forty benefits for reciting the aforesaid *durūd sharīf* which have been established and proven from authentic Ahādīth.[116] Here I will mention but a few, which apply to a person who has sincere love for the Messenger of Allāh 鏾, who respects the Messenger of Allāh 鏾 more than the world and everything that it contains, who stays far away from the company of those who try to belittle, degrade, or insult the Messenger of Allāh 鏾 in any shape or form, who shys away from those who try to prevent the remembrance of the Messenger of Allāh 鏾, who despises the antagonists of the Messenger of Allāh 鏾 (who are, in fact, the enemies of Allāh the Exalted). If such a person, who has in him all these qualities, recites this *durūd sharīf* with sincere love and devotion after the Jumu'ah prayer, whilst facing the illumined city of Madinah[117] and having his arms folded, then he shall receive the following benefits and blessings, and others besides:

---

[116] These benefits and virtues that the author alludes to have been extensively documented in many books on *salawāt* such as Sayyidī al-Imām Yūsuf ibn Ismā'īl an-Nabhānī's celebrated masterpiece *Sa'ādatud Dārayn fis Salāhi 'alā Sayyidil Kawnayn*.

[117] The direction of Madinah the Illumined is slightly towards the left of the direction of the Qibla in the United Kingdom.

❖ Allāh will shower three thousand blessings upon the person who recites this *durūd*.

❖ Allāh will send His salutations upon him two thousand times.

❖ Five thousand good deeds shall be written in his Book of Deeds.

❖ Five thousand of his sins shall be wiped away.

❖ He shall be elevated five thousand ranks.

❖ The Messenger of Allāh 🕌 shall shake hands with such a person on the Day of Reckoning.

❖ The forehead of this person will testify (in writing) that he is not a hypocrite.

❖ It shall also be written on his forehead that he is freed from the fire of Hell.

❖ Allāh Most High shall resurrect him amongst the martyrs on the Day of Resurrection.

❖ The wealth and prosperity of such a person shall increase.

❖ His children, grandchildren, and great-grandchildren will be a source of divine blessing [*barakāt*].

❖ He shall overcome (all obstacles) and be victorious over his antagonists.

❖ One day he will behold the blessed the Messenger of Allāh 🕌 in his dream.

❖ He shall pass away from this world in the state of faith [*īmān*].

❖ The intercession [*shafā'at*] of the Messenger of Allāh ﷺ shall be necessary [*wajib*] for him on the Day of Resurrection.

❖ Allāh, the All-Compassionate One, shall be pleased with him such that He shall never be displeased with him.

❖ People will love him from the depths of their hearts.[118]

[Here ends *al-Wazīfat al-Karīmah* by Shaykh al-Islām, Imām Ahmad Ridā Khān al-Qādirī ﷺ. The following salutations were compiled by the author's beloved grandson, al-Mufassir al-A'zam Shaykh Ibrāhīm Ridā Khān "Jīlānī Miyā" ﷺ (d. 1385/1965).]

(1) This *durūd sharīf* should be read 100 times after the Fajr prayer to increase the supplicant's prestige, and power, and to safeguard him from his opponents:

يَا عَزِيْزُ صَلِّ وَ سَلِّمْ وَ بَارِكْ عَلَى النَّبِىِّ الْعَزِيْزِ الْمُعِزِّ الْأَعَزِّ وَ عَلى آلِهٖ وَ اَصْحَابِهِ الْمُعَزَّزِيْنَ۔اَللّٰهُمَّ عَزِّزْنِيْ بِالْإِيْمَانِ وَحُسْنِ الْعَمَلِ وَ عَافِيَةِ الدَّائِمَةِ وَ حُسْنِ الْعَاقِبَةِ فِى الْأُمُوْرِ كُلِّهَا وَ هَبْ لَنَا ذُرِّيَّةً طَيِّبَةً إِنَّكَ سَمِيْعُ الدُّعَاءِ۔اللهُ رَبِّىْ لَا شَرِيْكَ لَهٗ

118 See Mālik al-'Ulamā 'Allāma Zafr ad-Dīn al-Biharī's *Hayāt-e A'lāhadrat*, vol. 3/pp. 46-47.

Yā 'Azīzu Salli wa Sallim wa Bārik 'alan Nabiyyil
'Azīzil Mu'izzil A'izzi wa 'alā Alihi wa Ashābihil
Mu'azzazīna. Allāhuma 'az-zizni bil Imāni wa
Husnil 'Amali wa Afiyatid Dāimati wa Husnil
Aqibati fil Umūri kulliha wa hab lana Dhurriyyatan
Tayyibatan Innaka Samī'ud Du'ā. Allāhu Rabbi lā
Sharīk lah.

O All-Mighty One, bestow Your salutations,
benedictions, and blessings upon the dearly
beloved Prophet, the honored, the most exalted,
and upon his noble Family and his illustrious
Companions. O Allāh! Strengthen me with faith
[*īmān*], good deeds, perpetual well-being, and a
good end to all my affairs, and bestow pious
children upon me. Verily, You are the answerer of
supplications. My Lord is Allāh; He has no partner.

(3) This *durūd sharīf* should be read 100 times after the
Zuhr prayer to increase the supplicant's wealth and faith
[*īmān*]; his work will also be full of divine blessings
[*barakāt*].

يَا كَرِيْمُ صَلِّ عَلَى النَّبِيِّ الْكَرِيْمِ مَعْدَنِ الْجُوْدِ
وَالْكَرَمِ وَ آلِهِ الْكِرَامِ وَابْنِهِ الْكَرِيْمِ وَعَبْدِهِ الْمُكَرَّمِ
وَ بَارِكْ وَ سَلِّمْ اَللَّهُمَّ أَكْرِمْ عَلَيْنَا بِكَرَمِكَ الْعَظِيْمِ

Yā Karīmu Salli 'alan Nabiyyil Karīmi Ma'dinil Jūdi
wal Karami wa Alihil Kirāmi wabnihil Karīmi wa

'Abdihil Mukarrami wa Bārik wa Sallim. Allāhumma Akrim 'alayna bi Karamik al-'Adhīm.

O Most Generous One, bestow Your salutations, mercy, and blessings upon the bountiful Prophet, the source of generosity and nobility, and upon his venerable Family and his noble son and his ennobled slave.[119] O Allāh, honor us with Your copious generosity.

(4) This *durūd sharīf* should be read 100 times after the 'Asr prayer for victory over the supplicant's adversaries, and to thwart the evil of those who conspire against him.

$$ يَا جَبَّارُ صَلِّ عَلَى سَيِّدِ الْقَاهِرِيْنَ قَاتِلِ الْمُشْرِكِيْنَ
دَافِعِ الْحَاسِدِيْنَ وَ آلِهِ وَ صَحْبِهِ اَجْمَعِيْنَ اَللّٰهُمَّ اقْهَرْ
عَلَى اَعْدَائِنَا بِقَهْرِكَ الْعَظِيْمِ يَا قَهَّارُ $$

Yā Jabbāru salli 'alā Sayiddil Qāhirīna Qātilil mushrikīna Dāfi'il hāsidīna wa Alihi wa Sahbihi Ajma'īn. Allāhumm'aqhar 'alā A'dā'ina bi Qahrikal 'Adhīmi Yā Qah'hāru!

---

[119] According to a live session answer given on February 19, 2012, by our spiritual mentor, Tāj al-Sharī'ah Muftī Muhammad Akhtar Ridā Khān al-Qādirī al-Azharī (may Allāh preserve him), this passage alludes to al-Ghawth al-A'zam Sayyidunā ash-Shaykh Muhyid'dīn 'Abd al-Qādir al-Jīlānī ﷺ.

O All-Compelling One, bestow Your salutations upon the liege-lord of the victorious, vanquisher of the idolaters, repeller of the envious, and upon his exalted Family and his glorious Companions. O Allāh, subdue our antagonists with the might of Your subdual. O Irresistible Subduer!

(5) This *durūd sharīf* should be read 100 times after the Maghrib prayer:

يَا سَتَّارُ صَلِّ عَلَى سِتْرِكَ الْجَمِيْلِ وَ آلِهِ وَ صَحْبِهِ وَ بَارِكْ وَ سَلِّمْ اَللّٰهُمَّ اسْتُرْنَا بِسِتْرِكَ الْجَمِيْلِ فَلَمْ اَزَلْ بِسِتْرِكَ الْجَمِيْلِ الْمُزَمِّلِ الْمُدَّثِّرِ مَسْتُوْرًا مُزَمَّلًا مُدَّثَّرًا اِلَى يَوْمِ الْقِيَامَةِ

Yā Sattāru Salli 'alā Sitrikal Jamīli wa Alihi wa Sahbihi wa Bārik wa Sallim. Allāhuma-sturna bi Sitrikal Jamīli fa-lam Azal bi-Sitrikal Jamīlil Muzzammilil Muddath-thiri Mastūran Muzzammilan Muddath-thiran ilā Yawmil Qiyāmah.

O Veiler of faults! Send Your salutations, mercy, and blessings upon Your beautiful veil (our liege-lord Muhammad, who serves as a veil and protects us from going astray and covers over our sins on the Day of Judgment through his intercession), and his Family and his Companions. O Veiler of faults! Veil us with Your beautiful veil so that I remain protected by Your beautiful veil until the Day of Judgment.

(6) This *durūd sharīf* should be read 100 times after the 'Ishā prayer for the preservation of the supplicant's life, property and to attain divine blessings [*barakāt*]:

يَا غَفَّارُ صَلِّ عَلَى شَفِيعِ الْمُذْنِبِيْنَ وَ آلِهِ وَ صَحْبِهِ
اَجْمَعِيْنَ رَبِّ اغْفِرْ لِيْ وَلِوَالِدَىَّ وَ لِجَمِيْعِ الْمُؤْمِنِيْنَ
وَالْمُؤْمِنَاتِ لَا اِلٰهَ اِلَّا اَنْتَ سُبْحَانَكَ اِنِّيْ كُنْتُ مِنَ
الظَّالِمِيْنَ

Yā Ghaffāru Salli alā Shafi'il mudhnibīna wa Alihi wa Sahbihi ajma'īna Rabbighfirli wa li-Wālidayya wali jami'il Mu'minīna wal Mu'mināti lā ilāha illa Anta Subhānaka innī kuntu minadh-Dhālimīn.

O All-Forgiving One, bestow Your salutations upon the Intercessor of the Sinners and upon his Family and all his Companions. O Allāh, forgive me and my parents and all the believing men and women. There is no deity save You, glory be to You! Verily, I was mistaken.

(7) *Durūd al-Fadl al-Azīm* ("Salutations of Excellence and Majesty") should be read 100 times a day. It is not restricted to a particular time or place, and guarantees a tremendous increase in divine blessings [*barakāt*], as well

as immense reward and protection against all [harmful] things:

يَا ذَا الْفَضْلِ الْعَظِيْمِ صَلِّ عَلٰى فَضْلِكَ الْعَظِيْمِ وَ
آلِهِ وَ صَحْبِهٖ وَ بَارِكْ وَ سَلِّمْ تَفَضَّلْ عَلَيْنَا بِفَضْلِكَ
الْعَظِيْمِ

Yā Dhal fadlil ʿadhīmi salli alā fadlikal adhīmi wa ālihi wa sahbihi wa bārik wa sallim tafaddal ʿalayna bi fadlikal adhīm.

O Possessor of Magnificent Excellence, bestow Your blessings upon Your gracious and exalted Prophet,[120] and upon his Family and his Companions. O Allāh, bestow Your favors upon us through the grace of Your favored Prophet.

(8) *Durūd al-Rahmah* ("Salutations of Divine Mercy") should also be recited 100 times a day. It is not restricted to any particular time or place, and contains unfathomable divine blessings [*barakāt*] for the reciter:

يَا رَحْمٰنُ يَا رَحِيْمُ صَلِّ وَ سَلِّمْ وَ بَارِكْ عَلٰى رَحْمَةٍ
لِّلْعَالَمِيْنَ رَاحَةِ الْمُؤْمِنِيْنَ الرَّءُوْفِ الرَّحِيْمِ وَ آلِهٖ وَ

---

[120] The word Prophet [*Nabī*] does not appear in this Arabic supplication. However, it was added to the English translation of the said *duʿā* to accurately convey its general meaning, chiefly because the Messenger of Allāh ﷺ is being referred to obliquely as the Lord's *fadlikal adhīm* (literally "greatest grace" [upon His creation]).

صَحْبِهِ وَ اَوْلِيَآئِهِ اَجْمَعِيْنَ وَ عَلَيْنَا مَعَهُمْ بِرَحْمَتِكَ
يَا اَرْحَمَ الرَّاحِمِيْنَ

Yā Rahmānu Yā Rahīmu salli wa sallim wa bārik
alā Rahmatil lil 'ālamīna Rāhatil Mu'minīn ar
Ra'ūfir Rahīmi wa ālihi wa sahbihi wa awlīyā'ihi
ajma'īna wa 'alayna ma'ahum bi-Rahmatika Yā
Arhamar Rāhimīn.

O All-Merciful One! O All-Compassionate One!
Bestow Your blessings upon the Mercy to the
Worlds, the solace of the believers, the
compassionate Prophet, and upon his Family and
his Companions and his allies and upon those of us
who follow them. O All-Merciful, All-
Compassionate Lord.

Formulae nine to fourteen have been excerpted from
Fadā'il Durūd Sharīf [The Virtues of Sending Blessings
upon the Prophet ﷺ].[121] This book is a compilation of
different articles written by al-Mufassir al-A'zam Shaykh
Ibrāhīm Ridā Khān "Jīlānī Miyā" ؓ that originally
appeared in the popular monthly magazine *Mahnama
'Alāhadrat* ؓ. This publication has been in circulation for
more than fifty years, and enjoys a wide-readership. The
Grand Muftī of Holland, Hadrat Muftī 'Abd al-Wajīd al-
Qādirī, collated these formulae of *Durūd* in a book entitled

---

[121] *Fadā'il Durūd Sharīf*, pp. 104-107.

Fadā'il Durūd Sharīf. He is a disciple [*murīd*] and deputy [*khalīfah*] of "Jīlānī Miyā" ﷺ.

(9) A meritorious excerpt from *Fadā'il Durūd Sharīf*:

رَبَّنَا هَبْ لَنَا مِنْ اَزْوَاجِنَا وَ ذُرِّيَّاتِنَا قُرَّةَ اَعْيُنٍ وَّاجْعَلْنَا لِلْمُتَّقِيْنَ اِمَامًا۔رَبِّ اَعُوْذُ بِكَ مِنْ هَمَزَاتِ الشَّيَاطِيْنِ وَ اَعُوْذُ بِكَ رَبِّ اَنْ يَّحْضُرُوْنِ۔رَبِّ اَعُوْذُ بِكَلِمَاتِ اللهِ التَّآمَّاتِ مِنْ شَرِّ مَا خَلَقَ۔ سَلَا مٌ عَلَى اِبْرَاهِيْمَ سَلَا مٌ عَلى مُوْسٰى وَ هَارُوْنَ سَلَا مٌ عَلَى اِلْيَاسِيْنَ سَلَا مٌ عَلَى الْمُرْسَلِيْنَ سَلَا مٌ عَلَى نُوْحٍ فِي الْعَالَمِيْنَ سَلَا مٌ قَوْلًا مِّنْ رَّبٍّ رَّحِيْمٍ۔ سَلَا مٌ هِيَ حَتَّى مَطْلَعِ الْفَجْرِ بِحُرْمَةِ الٓمّ الٓمّص كهيٰعص، طسّم، طسّ، حٰمٓ عسٓقٓ، نٓ، يسٓ، طٰهٰ، قٓ، الٓمّرٰ، يَا رِجَالَ الْغَيْبِ يَا شَيْخُ عَبْدَ الْقَادِرِ جِيْلَانِيٍّ شَيْئًا لِلّٰهِ

Rabbanā hab lanā min azw ājinā wa dhurriyātinā qurrata a'yuniw waj'alnā lil muttaqina imāmā. Rabbi a'ūdhubika min hamazātish shayatini wa a'ūdhubika Rabbi ay yahdurūni. Rabbi a'ūdhu bi kalimātillāhit tammāti min sharri ma khalaq. Salāmun alā Ibrahīm, Salāmun alā Mūsa wa Harūn. Salāmun alā Ilyasīn. Salāmum alal Mursalīn. Salāmun alā Nūhin fil ālamīn. Salāmun Qaulam mir Rabbir rahīm. Salāmun hiya hatta matla'il Fajar. Bihur mati Alif Lām Mīm, Alif Lām Sād, Kāf Hā Yā

A'in Sād, Tā Sīn Mīm, Tā Sīn, Hā Mīm, A'in Sīn Qāf,
Hā Mīm, Nūn, Yāsīn, Tā Hā, Qāf, Alif Lām Mīm Ra.
Yā rijālal ghayb. Yā Shaykh 'Abd al-Qādir al-Jīlānī
Shay an lil lāh.

Our Lord, grant us from our wives and children
such who are a source of coolness of our eyes, and
make us the leaders [*imāms*] for the righteous.[122] My
Lord, I seek refuge in You from the whisperings of
demonic beings. My Lord, I seek refuge in You
from their presence around me. Lord, I seek refuge
with Your perfect words from the evil of what You
have created. Peace be upon Ibrahīm; peace be
upon Mūsa and Harūn. Peace be upon Ilyas; peace
be upon all of the Messengers. Peace be upon Nūh
among all beings. Peace—a word from the Lord.
Peace until the rising of the dawn. Through the
sanctify of [the Qurānic letters] Alif Lām Mīm, Alif
Lām Sād, Kāf Hā Yā 'Ayn Sād, Tā Sīn Mīm, Tā Sīn,
Hā Mīm, 'Ayn Sīn Qāf, Hā Mīm, Nūn, Yāsīn, Tā Hā,
Qāf, Alif Lām Mīm Ra.[123] O men of the unseen

---

[122] The first part of this salutation is a powerful supplication [*du'ā*] from
Sūrah al-Furqān, 25:74.

[123] Allāh, the Sublime and Exalted, begins many Chapters of the Holy
Qur'ān with these mysterious Arabic letters. Their meaning is known
only to Him. Yet the reward for reciting even one of these Qur'ānic
letters is immense! Mullā 'Alī al-Qārī ﷺ in his *Fayd al-Mu'īn 'alā Jam'il-
Arba'īn fī Fadl al-Qur'ān al-Mubīn* reported on the authority of Abdullāh
ibn Mas'ūd ﷺ that the Messenger of Allāh ﷺ said: "Whosoever reads a
single letter of the Qur'ān will have ten rewards. I do not say that *alif*

[assist me]! O Shaykh 'Abd al-Qādir al-Jīlānī, assist me in this matter for the sake of Allāh![124]

(10) A meritorious excerpt from *Fadā'il Durūd Sharīf*:

يَا عَزِيزُ صَلِّ عَلَى النَّبِيِّ الْعَزِيزِ الْمُعِزِّ الْأَعَزِّ وَ
آلِهِ وَ صَحْبِهِ الْمُعَزَّزِيْنَ وَ بَارِكْ وَ سَلِّمْ، اَللّٰهُمَّ
عَزِّزْنِيْ بِإِعْزَازِ فَضْلِكَ الْعَظِيْمِ فِى الدُّنْيَا وَالْآخِرَةِ

Yā 'Azizu Salli 'alan Nabiyyil 'Azīzil Mu'izzil A'azz wa Ālihi wa Sahbihil Mu'azzazīn wa Bārik wa Sallim Allāhumma 'Azzizni bi-I'zāzi Fadlikal 'Adhīm fi'd Dunyā wa'l Ākhirah

O Almighty One! Bestow Your salutations, blessings, and benedictions upon the powerful, strong, and respected Prophet, and upon his exalted Family and dearest Companions—blessings of peace. O Allāh! Strengthen and fortify me

---

lām mīm is one letter, but rather *alif* is a letter, *lām* is a letter, and *mīm* is a letter." (This sound Hadīth was narrated by at-Tirmidhī.)

[124] In *Barakāt al-Imdād li Ahlil-Istimdād* [The Validity of Saying Yā Rasūl Allāh ﷺ], the erudite author (Imām Ahmad Ridā Khān ﷺ) provides an irrefutable explanation as to why seeking assistance from the Prophets and Sufi saints is permissible in Islam. This book is a must-read for Muslims in general and those who may have doubts or misgivings about seeking a means [*wasīla*] in particular. It has been translated into English by Shaykh 'Abd al-Hādī al-Qādirī Radāwī in his *Thesis of Imam Ahmad Raza* ﷺ.

through Your divine grace in this world and the next.

(11) A meritorious excerpt from *Fadā'il Durūd Sharīf*:

$$\text{يَا كَرِيْمُ صَلِّ عَلَى النَّبِيِّ الْكَرِيْمِ وَ آلِهِ الْكِرَامِ وَابْنِهِ}$$
$$\text{الْكَرِيْمِ وَ عَبْدِهِ الْمُكَرَّمِ وَ بَارِكْ وَ سَلِّمِ اللَّهُمَّ اَكْرِمْ}$$
$$\text{عَلَيْنَا بِكَرَمِكَ الْعَظِيْمِ فِى الدُّنْيَا وَالْآخِرَةِ}$$

Yā Karīmu Salli 'alan Nabiyyil Karīm wa Ālihil Kirām wabnihil Karīm wa 'abdihil Mukarram wa Bārik wa Sallim Allāhumma Akrim 'alaynā bi-Karamikal 'Adhīm fi'd Dunyā wa'l Ākhirah

O Ever-Generous One! Bestow Your salutations, blessings, and benedictions upon the august Prophet, and his venerable Family and his noble son and his ennobled slave.[125] O Allāh! Honor us with Your divine generosity in this world and the next.

---

[125] According to a live session answer given on February 19, 2012, by our spiritual mentor, Tāj al-Sharī'ah Muftī Muhammad Akhtar Ridā Khān al-Qādirī al-Azharī (may Allāh preserve him), this passage alludes to al-Ghawth al-A'zam Sayyidunā ash-Shaykh Muhyid'dīn 'Abd al-Qādir al-Jīlānī ﷺ.

(12) A meritorious excerpt from *Fadā'il Durūd Sharīf*:

يَا جَبَّارُ وَ يَا مُذِلَّ كُلِّ جَبَّارٍ عَنِيْدٍ صَلِّ عَلَى حِصْنِنَا وَ حَصِيْنِنَا وَ سَيِّدِنَا مُحَمَّدٍ وَّ آلِهِ وَ صَحْبِهِ وَ بَارِكْ وَ سَلِّمْ وَ اقْهَرْ بِهَا عَلَى اَعْدَاءِ الْإِسْلَام وَ الْمُسْلِمِيْنَ وَ تَحَصَّنَا وَ احْفَظْنَا مِنْ كَيْدِهِمْ وَ شَرِّهِم

Yā Jabbāru wa Yā Mudhilla Kulli Jabbārin 'Anīd Salli 'Ala Hisninā wa Hasīninā wa Sayyidinā Muhammadiw wa Ālihi wa Sahbihi wa Bārik wa Sallim wa'qhar bihā 'ala A'dā'il Islām wa'l Muslimīn wa Tahassanā wa'hfadhnā min kaydihim wa sharrihim

O All-Compelling One and Requiter, Who debases every obstinate tyrant! Bestow Your salutations, blessings, and benedictions upon our refuge and liege-lord Muhammad, and upon his Family and Companions. And subjugate the antagonists of Islam and protect the Muslims, and fortify us, and protect us from the plotting and treachery of the non-believers.

(13) A meritorious excerpt from *Fadā'il Durūd Sharīf*:

يَا سَتَّارُ صَلِّ عَلَى سِتْرِكَ الْجَمِيْلِ وَ آلِهِ وَ صَحْبِهِ وَ بَارِكْ وَ سَلِّمْ اَللّٰهُمَّ يَا سَتَّارُ اسْتُرْنَا بِسِتْرِكَ الْجَمِيْلِ فِى الدُّنْيَا وَالْآخِرَةِ

Yā Sattāru Salli 'alā Sitrika'l Jamīl wa Ālihi wa Sahbihi wa Bārik wa Sallim Allāhumma Yā Sattāru Usturnā bi-Sitrika'l Jamīl fi'd Dunyā wa'l Ākhirah

O Veiler of faults! Send Your salutations, blessings, and benedictions upon Your most beautiful veil (our liege-lord Muhammad, who serves as a veil and protects us from going astray and covers over our sins on the Day of Judgment through his intercession), and upon his Family and his Companions. O Veiler of faults! Veil us with Your most beautiful veil in this world and the next.

(14) A meritorious excerpt from *Fadā'il Durūd Sharīf*:

يَا غَفَّارُ صَلِّ عَلَى رَسُوْلِنَا الْمُغَفَّرِ وَ اِخْوَانِهِ الْمَعْصُوْمِيْنَ وَ آلِهِ وَ اَصْحَابِهِ الْمَحْفُوْظِيْنَ وَ بَارِكْ وَ سَلِّمْ. اَللّٰهُمَّ يَا غَفَّارَ الذُّنُوْبِ وَ يَا سَتَّارَ الْعُيُوْبِ اِغْفِرْ ذُنُوْبَنَا وَاسْتُرْ عُيُوْبَنَا اِنَّكَ اَنْتَ الْغَفَّارُ وَالسَّتَّارُ بِرَحْمَتِكَ يَا اَرْحَمَ الرَّاحِمِيْنَ

Yā Ghaffāru Salli 'alā Rasūlinal Mughaffar wa Ikhwānihi'l Ma'sūmīn wa Ālihi wa Ashābihi al-Mahfūdhīn wa Bārik wa Sallim Allāhumma Yā Ghaffār-adh-Dhunūb wa Yā Sattār-al-'Uyūb Ighfir Dhunūbanā wa'stur 'Uyūbanā Innaka Anta'l Ghaffār wa's Sattār bi-Rahmatika Yā Arham ar-Rāhimīn

O All-Forgiving One! Send Your salutations, blessings, and benedictions upon our infallible Messenger and his sinless brothers (the Prophets of Allāh), and upon his inviolable Family and Companions. O Allāh! You are the Forgiver of all sins and the Veiler of all defects! Forgive our sins and veil our defects. Verily, You are the Forgiver and the Veiler. O Most Merciful One! You are the Most Merciful of those who show mercy.

The Guidebook of Blessings

By Muhammad Kalīm al-Qādirī

Dalā'il al-Khayrāt [The Guidebook of Blessings] is a compendium of blessings and peace upon the Prophet ﷺ [*durūd sharīf*]. It was compiled by the shaykh, the scholar, the gnostic, the pious friend of Allāh, the blessing of Marrakesh,[126] Imām Abū 'Abdullāh Muhammad ibn Sulayman ibn Abī Bakr al-Jazūlī al-Simlalī al-Hasanī ﷺ. He was born in the city of Jazūla in the Sūs area of present-day Morocco. Here he studied the Holy Qur'ān before embarking on a quest for knowledge that took him to Fes where he met the gnostic Sayyidī Ahmad al-Zarrūq ﷺ, and studied at Madrasat as-Saffarīn. To this day, visitors to this prestigious Islamic institute are shown his room. He also sought Sacred Knowledge in the *Maghrib*,[127] and sat with teachers from Marrakesh, Tlemcen and Tunisia. He spent several decades in Makkah the Ennobled, Madinah the Illumined, and Jerusalem. His travels took him to Egypt and Tripoli, too. He was initiated into the Shādhilī Tarīqah by Sharīf Abū 'Abdullāh Muhammad ibn Amghar ﷺ.

---

[126] Marrakesh is a city in Morocco.
[127] The region of Northwest Africa that includes five countries: Morocco, Algeria, Tunisia, Libya, and Mauritania.

Imām al-Jazūlī remained in seclusion [*khalwa*] for fourteen years. Upon returning to Fez, he was ordained as a Shaykh of the Tarīqah, and completed *Dalā'il al-Khayrāt wa Shawāriq al-Anwār fī Dhikr al-Salāti 'alan Nabiyy al-Mukhtār* ﷺ [The Guidebook of Blessings and Enlightenment that comes from Invoking the Chosen Prophet ﷺ in Prayer]. He then went to Safi where numerous followers gathered around him. Unfortunately, the governor of Safi felt obliged to expel him, and later poisoned him. This tragic event ultimately resulted in his martyrdom [*shahādah*] in 870/1465. It is said that he died whilst performing the ritual prayer. His body was exhumed in 1541, and transferred to Marrakesh. Imām al-Jazūlī's mortal frame had not decomposed seventy-six years after his death.

Commenting on the *Dalā'il al-Khayrāt*, Imām al-Sayyid al-Murtadā al-Zabīdī ﷺ said: "Out of all the manuals written on *salawāt*, Allāh granted it the greatest popular appeal and acclaim, which no other book has been given. The elite and the common folk alike have expressed a deep and abiding love for this book. They have also supplemented the book by writing commentaries and adding footnotes to it. This [worldwide acceptance] is due to the sincere intention of its author, and his heartfelt expression of love for the Messenger ﷺ."[128]

Similarly, Shaykh Hājī Khalīfah states: "The book is a sign from the signs of Allāh in being one of the best manuals collating formulae in sending salutations upon

---

[128] Imām an-Nabhānī's *Sa'ādah al-Dārayn*, p. 33.

the Messenger 🌸. People passionately read it from the far corners of the earth."[129]

Imām an-Nabhānī 🕮 quotes al-'Ārif Billāh[130] Imām Ahmad al-Sāwī al-Misrī's 🕮 commentary on the *salawāt* of al-Qutb Shaykh al-Dardirī 🕮 to explain why this magnificent book (*Dalā'il al-Khayrāt*) was compiled and what inspired Imām al-Jazūlī to gift such a manual to this Community:

"One day Imām al-Jazūlī went to perform his ritual ablution from a nearby well, as the time for the prescribed prayer was approaching. However, he was unable to find a means by which to draw the water from the well. In the midst of this difficulty, he was seen by a young girl who called out from overhead: 'You're the one people extol! Yet you can't even draw water out of a well?' So she came down and spat into the water, which welled up until it overflowed and spilled across the ground. Imām al-Jazūlī made his ritual ablution, and then turned to her and said: 'I adjure you to tell me how you reached this station [*maqām*].' She replied: 'By sending blessings and salutations upon him 🌸, whom beasts lovingly followed as he walked through the wilderness.' Imām al-Jazūlī thereupon vowed to compose his *Dalā'il al-Khayrāt wa Shawāriq al-Anwār fi Dhikris Salāh 'alan Nabiyy al-Mukhtār* [The Guidebook of Blessings and Enlightenment that

---

[129] *Kashf al-Dhunun*, vol. 1/p. 759.
[130] *Al-Ārif Billāh*: "The Gnostic of Allāh."

comes from Invoking the Chosen Prophet ﷺ in Prayer]."[131]

Imām an-Nabhānī ﷺ further writes: "Our Master, Shaykh al-Sunnah, Imām Hasan al-'Adawī al-Misrī, said in his commentary *Bulūgh al-Masarrāt 'alā Dalā'il al-Khayrāt* that: 'It is a sufficient proof of the blessings of this book that its perimeter of acceptance and fame has reached an unprecedented extent that astounds the mind… and why not? Indeed, some of the gnostics have received this manual directly from the Chief of the Envoys ﷺ…'"[132]

Whilst giving biographical information about Shaykh al-Siddiq al-Filalī ﷺ in *Salwat al-Anfās*, Imām Sayyid Muhammad ibn Ja'far al-Kattānī ﷺ said: "He (Shaykh al-Siddiq) was unlettered, yet he memorized the *Dalā'il al-Khayrāt* by heart. He said that the Messenger of Allāh ﷺ taught him the *Dalā'il* through a series of dreams. The Messenger ﷺ would appear in his dream, and teach him to recite some of the *salawāt* from this book. When Shaykh al-Siddiq woke up, he found that he had memorized that portion of the book. This process continued until he had memorized the entire *Dalā'il*."

The great Reviver [*mujaddid*] of Islam, al-'Ārif Billāh al-Qutb, Imām Ahmad Ridā Khān al-Qādirī ﷺ, and his descendants including our spiritual mentor, al-'Ārif Billāh Tāj al-Sharī'ah, Muftī Muhammad Akhtar Ridā Khān al-Qādirī al-Azharī (may Allāh preserve him), have shown a passionate bond to this seminal masterpiece. In point of

---

[131] *Al-Dalalat al-Wadihat 'alā Dalā'il al-Khayrāt*, p. 61.
[132] Ibid., p. 48.

fact, Hadrat Tāj al-Sharī'ah did not permit his weakened eyesight to obstruct his memorization of the *Dalā'il* in its entirety; such was his love for this guidebook of blessings. In July 2010, we had the honor of sitting at the feet of our Shaykh and listening to portions of his recitation in the City of the Beloved ﷺ. All praise belongs to Allāh alone, the Lord of the worlds! We were blessed to receive permission [*ijāzah*] to read this manual of *salawāt* and teach it to others from our Shaykh, the Chief Judge of India, and from al-Muhaddīth al-Kabīr Shaykh Diyā al-Mustafā al-Qādirī, the great Hadīth master and Islamic jurist [*faqīh*] of this age (may Allāh preserve them both).

Reading the *Dalā'il* fills the soul with light [*nūr*], increases divine insight, and opens the heart to the spiritual realm of which the greatest benefit is increasing our love for the Beloved of Allāh ﷺ. In a letter to Mawlānā Tājammul Hudā Sāhib, the great gnostic and founder of al-Jami'ah al-Ashrafiyyah in Mubarakpur (India), Hāfiz al-Millat [The Guardian of the Nation] Shaykh 'Abd al-'Azīz ﷺ, gave the following guidelines for reciting the *Dalā'il al-Khayrāt*: "One should make a sincere intention to recite it at a fixed time [each day]; it only takes fifteen minutes [to read a daily *hizb* of the *ahzab* apportioned according to the days in the week]. Among the blessings of the *Dalā'il al-Khayrāt Sharīf* is that anyone who makes a steadfast resolution to recite it daily without fail shall not miss his recitation. One should apply perfume before reciting it. It is also from its blessings that anyone who is persistent in its recitation shall have his affairs completed from the unseen realm and shall receive spiritual openings... to recite it whilst in the state of ritual ablution [*wudū'*] and to apply perfume is from its etiquettes..."[133]

Ḥāfiz al-Millat himself was always punctual in his daily recital of *Dalā'il al-Khayrāt* up to his last breath. His love and attachment to it was to such an extent that in his latter days when he became physically too weak to perform the recital himself, he would appoint someone from his students or disciples to recite the litany aloud, whilst he would listen to it.[134] His ardent love for this masterwork bore fruit at the time of his union [*wisāl*]. As the reader already knows, Ḥāfiz al-Millat made the following declaration about the *Dalā'il al-Khayrāt* in the aforementioned letter to Mawlānā Tājammul Hudā Sahib: "Anyone who makes a steadfast resolution to recite it daily without fail shall not miss his recitation." Undoubtedly, Ḥāfiz al-Millat was blessed with a miracle [*karāmāh*] from Allāh, the Exalted, for his faith and steadfast devotion. On the day of his *wisāl*, his highly esteemed and renowned student, al-Muhaddīth al-Kabīr Shaykh Diyā al-Mustafā al-Qādirī (may Allāh preserve him), recited portions of the *Dalā'il al-Khayrāt* at the side of his body after the Fajr prayer.[135]

This righteous scholar ﷺ inculcated the love of Allāh and His Messenger ﷺ in his students and disciples by teaching them to hold fast to *salawāt*, especially the daily recitation of the *Dalā'il al-Khayrāt*. We had the good fortune of witnessing one of his celebrated students, Shaykh

---

[133] *Hayāt-e Hafiz-e Millat*, pp. 482-483.
[134] Ibid., p. 538.
[135] Ibid., p. 815.

Arshad al-Qādirī ❧ (d. 2002/1422) also known as the Leader of the Pen [*Ra'īs al-Qalam*], spend a significant amount of his time engrossed in the recitation of the *Dalā'il al-Khayrāt* during his visit to the United Kingdom.[136] He would keep olive oil and kohl beside him whilst reciting the *Dalā'il*. Then he would give this oil to those who were afflicted with illnesses, and it would cure them by the grace of Allāh Almighty. In conclusion, the veracity of this sublime book is evident from the number of miracles [*karāmāt*] that Allāh Most High has bestowed upon the lovers of His Beloved ❧.

May the Bountiful Lord grant us enabling success [*tawfīq*] to recite this extraordinary book, whose blessings are witnessed around the world, āmīn.

---

[136] Shaykh Arshad al-Qādirī ❧ had visited the United Kingdom (UK) on several occasions. His last visit to the UK was in 2000, just two years before his demise. May the Sublime Lord shower immense mercy on his blessed grave.

Biographies

IMĀM AHMAD RIDĀ KHĀN AL-QĀDIRĪ ﷺ

Imām Ahmad Ridā, more popularly known as A'lāhadrat, was born in 1272/1856. He was a renowned Hanafī scholar from Bareilly, India; and a child prodigy, who was educated at home by his esteemed father, 'Allāma Naqī 'Alī Khān ﷺ (d. 1297/1880). He completed the Dars-e Nizāmī syllabus studying a range of twenty-one Islamic sciences by the age of thirteen. In 1295/1878 and again in 1323/1905, Imām Ahmad undertook the pilgrimage to Makkah the Ennobled. On both occasions he received recognition from top-ranking scholars. During his first trip to the Holy City he received licenses and training from the Muftī of the Hanafī school, Shaykh 'Abd al-Rahmān al-Sirāj ﷺ, from the Shāfi'ī Imām, Shaykh Husayn Sālih ﷺ, and from the Muftī of the Shāfi'ī school and Chief Judge [Qādī al-Qudāt] of Makkah, Shaykh Ahmad ibn Zayni Dahlan ﷺ.

Among Imām Ahmad's greatest contributions to Islamic literature is without doubt *Kanz al-Īmān* [A Treasury of Faith], which is an authoritative translation of the Qur'ān into the Urdu language. Likewise his Arabic, Persian, and Urdu poetry is inspiring and beautiful,

143

especially *Mustafā Jān-e Rahmat* [Mustafā ☙ the Paragon of Mercy]. This poem in praise of the Chosen One ☙ is traditionally recited during religious celebrations such as the *Mawlid*,[137] not only in the Subcontinent, but also in other parts of the world. Those who have read his *al-Malfūz al-Sharīf* [Noble Utterances] will testify to his deep and abiding love for the Sufi saints [*awlīyā*], and the 'Ulamā of the *Ahl al-Sunnah wa al-Jamā'ah*. He also wrote a definitive masterpiece on the Prophet's knowledge of the unseen ☙ entitled, *al-Dawlah al-Makkiyyah bi'l Maddat al-Ghaybiyya* [The Makkan Realm on the Matter of the Unseen]. This monograph has received seventy-seven endorsements from the scholars of Hijaz, Yemen, Syria, and Egypt.

Imām Ahmad is regarded by many to be one of the most famous scholars in South Asia and a Renewer [*mujaddid*] of the 14th Islamic century AH. He was a preeminent theologian, Hanafī jurist, metaphysician, Hadīth expert, and heresiologist well known for three areas of research: (1) defending the honor of the Master of the Messengers ☙, (2) attacking blameworthy innovators

---

[137] *Mawlid*, also spelled *Mīlād*, is the celebration of Prophet Muhammad's ☙ birth on the 12th of Rabī' al-Awwal. The birthday of Allāh's Messenger ☙ is an official holiday in fifty-four Islamic countries, and a good innovation that merits reward. Wahhābīs cannot bear this custom and have banned it publicly in Saudi Arabia. It is also contested and condemned by Islamic seminaries closely affiliated with them such as the reformist Deoband school in India. For a brilliant defense of the *Mawlid* and the practice of standing [*qiyām*] during its commemoration, see Imām Ahmad's *The Elite Stand in Honour of the Chosen One* ☙.

who challenged the creed of the *Ahl al-Sunnah wa al-Jamā'ah*, and (3) delivering formal legal edicts [*fatāwā*] according to the clear and popular Hanafī legal school. In addition to all this, he was a prolific writer whose legal edicts were gathered into twelve encyclopedic volumes, and covered almost every science of his day. Carl W. Earnst and Bruce B. Lawrence accurately note that the devotional and pietist Barelwī school,[138] "champions practices that honor the Prophet and the Sufi saints."[139] This was Imām Ahmad's pedagogy and his enduring legacy to the Community of Sayyidunā Muhammad ﷺ.

Shaykh al-Islām Imām Ahmad Ridā Khān al-Qādirī ﷺ passed onto the Realm of Divine Beauty on a Friday, the 25th of Safar, 1340 AH (October 28, 1921). It was the exact time of the Jumu'ah Adhān.[140] His blessed mausoleum in the town of Bareilly, India is still a place of pious visitation for scholars and laymen alike. May the Sublime Lord have mercy on him and fill his grave with light, āmīn.

---

[138] Imām Ahmad ﷺ is highly revered as the leader of the *Ahl al-Sunnah wa al-Jamā'ah* in modern South Asian Islam; Islamicists tend to refer to his pedagogy as the Barelwī school due to his surname *al-Barelwī*, which indicates his place of birth [i.e., Bareilly, India]. However, the reader should note that opponents of the *Ahl al-Sunnah* use the word "Barelwī" in a derogatory sense to cast aspersions upon Imām Ahmad's school of thought.

[139] Carl W. Ernst and Bruce B. Lawrence, *Sufi Martyrs of Love: The Chishti Order in South Asia and Beyond* (New York: PALGRAVE MACMILLAN, 2002), p. 96.

[140] The Jumu'ah Adhān is the Friday call to prayer.

SHAYKH MUSTAFĀ RIDĀ KHĀN ﷺ

An eminent Muftī of the Indian Subcontinent and scholar par excellence, Shaykh Mustafā, also widely known as *al-Muftī al-A'zam* (or, "The Supreme Muftī of India"),[141] was born in Bareilly in 1310/1892. He was Imām Ahmad's younger son and the spiritual successor [*khalīfah*] of Sayyid Shāh Abu'l Husayn Ahmad an-Nūrī ﷺ of Marehra Sharīf. His primary education was obtained at Dār al-'Ulūm Manzar al-Islām (Bareilly), where he studied under some of the most distinguished scholars of his time, including his elder brother, *Hujjat al-Islām* (or, "The Proof of Islam") Shaykh Hāmid Ridā Khān al-Qādirī ﷺ, *Ustādh al-Asātidha* (or, "The Teacher of the Teachers") 'Allāma Shāh Raham Ilāhī Maglorī ﷺ, Shaykh al-'Ulamā Sayyid Bashīr Ahmad 'Aligarhī ﷺ, and *Shams al-'Ulamā* (or, "The Sun of the Scholars") Zahūr al-Hussain Rampurī ﷺ.

Shaykh Mustafā mastered thirty-six Islamic sciences by his eighteenth birthday. He was in the constant habit of praying and punctually performed the ritual prayers in congregation, even whilst traveling. His tongue was always moist with the remembrance of Allāh Most Pure [*dhikr*], especially when writing talismans for the masses that flocked to him. He became proficient in several subtle forms of Dhikr that are known to the elect, as well. He authored more than thirty books, including several

---

[141] Shaykh Mustafā ﷺ is considered by many highly distinguished *Mashāyikh* and 'Ulamā to be the Renewer [*mujaddid*] of the 15th Islamic century AH.

146

outstanding works on Islamic doctrine [*'aqīdah*] and jurisprudence [*fiqh*]. Allāh, the Sublime and Exalted, blessed him with a long life for the benefit of the Community; he was also blessed with the foreknowledge of his last hour. His physical body was laid to rest in the city of Bareilly in 1402/1981. May the Sublime Lord have mercy on him and fill his grave with light, āmīn.

SHAYKH IBRĀHĪM RIDĀ KHĀN ﷺ

Shaykh Ibrāhīm Ridā Khān ﷺ was a scholar of Qur'ānic exegesis, master of the Hadīth sciences, profound orator, and the foremost spokesperson for A'lāhadrat ﷺ. He was regarded by many to be the *Qamar al-'Ārifīn* (or, "The Satellite of the Gnostics") for he shined upon them whilst orbiting in their sacred space.[142] Not only was he declared the Pillar of the Commentators (*'Umdat al-Mufassirīn*), but also the Greatest Exegete of India (*al-Mufassir al-A'zam Hind*) for he proved to be the most knowledgeable scholar of the Magnificent Qur'ān in the Subcontinent, and a source of untold support and strength!

Shaykh Ibrāhīm was known for his piety, miracles, personal humility, and wisdom. He often said, "My own faults stop me from finding fault in others." And, "Piety is achieved through good character, not through filial ties." He left this mundane world in 1385/1965. May the Sublime Lord have mercy on him and fill his grave with light, āmīn.

---

[142] *Qamar* is an Arabic word that literally means "moon."

www.ingramcontent.com/pod-product-compliance
Lightning Source LLC
Chambersburg PA
CBHW051728040426
42447CB00008B/1024